BRAMALL HALL: the story of an Elizabethan manor house

To my mother
and in memory of my father

BRAMALL HALL

THE STORY OF AN ELIZABETHAN MANOR HOUSE

by

E. BARBARA DEAN

Published by the Recreation & Culture Division
Metropolitan Borough of Stockport

1977

Published by the Recreation & Culture Division
Metropolitan Borough of Stockport

ISBN 0 905164 06 7

Printed by John Bentley (Printers) Ltd
Halifax Road, Todmorden, Lancashire

Royalties from the sale of this book are being donated by the author to a
Bramall Hall Furnishings & Fabric Fund, set up for the acquisition of
items of special interest and the carrying out of appropriate conservation
work

CONTENTS

ILLUSTRATIONS

The jacket illustration shows the east front as it is today

FOREWORD

It gives me great pleasure to commend this history of Bramall Hall and the families who lived there.

Miss Dean has devoted most of her recent rare leisure time to this lovingly researched history of one of England's manor houses. History of such a house exemplifies in miniature the history of England, with each generation coming alive for us in turn.

I knew little of the history of my own family until this research was undertaken, and I remember with pleasure my first visit to Bramhall in 1950 and the feeling of continuity that it gave.

It is good to know that Bramall Hall is well looked after – formerly by the Hazel Grove & Bramhall Urban District Council and now by the Stockport Metropolitan Borough Council – and that the public is able to enjoy its unique features. I hope this book will give pleasure to many people who go to see the house and a greater insight into the lives of its occupants – all of them ordinary people like ourselves, who made their distinctive contribution to their own age.

David Davenport-Handley

Clipsham Hall
Rutland, Leicestershire

ACKNOWLEDGMENTS

The story of Bramall Hall, a house whose main features date from the reign of Queen Elizabeth I and whose beginnings could have been some two hundred years earlier, has been a fascinating study. The lecture notes and slide collection left by my father, Reginald Dean, first inspired the work and thereafter provided a firm basis for its continuance, though I am aware that research on such a subject could be endless. I also gratefully acknowledge my indebtedness to the following:

D. J. Davenport-Handley, J. A. Christie-Miller, Katharine M. H. Sidebottom, the late G. N. Carleton-Stiff, and the late Elsie A. Partington (for information concerning their respective families)

The former Hazel Grove & Bramhall Urban District Council and the present Stockport Metropolitan Borough Council (for access to minutes, correspondence etc., and for permissions in connection with the Burton MSS)

The officers of the above councils (for their assistance)

Gladys Lawton, honorary secretary of the Friends of Bramall Hall (for information concerning the society)

Marjorie Wrigley, Shirley Rudd, J. Fleming Andrew, and Bramhall and Stockport friends

The staff of the libraries I have visited, and particularly the staff of the Stockport Reference Library and of the Cheshire Record Office

Sir Walter Bromley-Davenport (for the wording of Dame Dorothy's lines on her Paradise Bed)

Extracts from the Diary of Charles Bellairs are quoted by courtesy of C. D. M. B. Alderson and R. G. B. Isherwood, present-day representatives of the Bellairs and Isherwood families.

Extracts from Davenport wills are quoted by permission of the Cheshire County Archivist; extracts from the sermon preached at the funeral of William Davenport, 1696, by permission of D. J. Davenport-

ACKNOWLEDGMENTS

Handley and the Cheshire County Archivist; extracts from the Barritt MS and Palmer MS D, by permission of the feoffees of Chetham's Library; extracts from the Torrington Diaries, by permission of C. B. Andrews and Messrs Eyre & Spottiswoode.

I am grateful to all who have given permission for the use of photographs. Sources of illustrations are as follows: Nos. 1, 12, collection of the late William Galloway; Nos. 2, 7, 8, 9, 10, photograph album of the late Dorothy Davenport-Belt (now the property of Stockport Metropolitan Borough Council); Nos. 3, 18, the former Hazel Grove & Bramhall Urban District Council; Nos. 4, 5, D. J. Davenport-Handley and Friends of Bramall Hall; No. 6, Sir Walter Bromley-Davenport and the former Hazel Grove & Bramhall Urban District Council; No. 11, J. A. Christie-Miller; Nos. 13, 14, 15, Katharine M. H. Sidebottom; Nos. 16, 17, executors of the late Elsie A. Partington; No. 19, Stockport Metropolitan Borough Council; No. 20, a press photograph; No. 21, *Stockport Express*.

E.B.D.

October, 1976

The poem on page 105 was
written by Samuel Andrew (of Hey,
Lees, Oldham) and published in the
Manchester City News, 28 May 1887,
under the title 'Ancestral Bramhall'.

CHRONOLOGICAL TABLE

Lords of the manor of Bramhall, with dates of entering into possession

Brun and Hacun (Saxon freemen)	Before 1066

Hamon de Massy (a follower of William the Conqueror)	c. 1070
Hamon (second Baron of Dunham Massey)	Date unknown
Matthew de Bromale	Temp. Henry II
Richard de Bromale (1)	c. 1277
Richard de Bromale (2)	c. 1326
Richard de Bromale (3)	Date unknown
Geoffrey de Bromale	Date unknown

John de Davenport (1)	c. 1370
Robert de Davenport	c. 1400
John de Davenport (2) (1419-1478)	1436
William Davenport (1) (1446-1528)	1478
William Davenport (2) (1472-1541)	1528
William Davenport (3) (1521-1576)	1541
William Davenport (4) (1543-1585)	1576
William Davenport (5) (c. 1563-c. 1639)	1585
William Davenport (6) (1584-1655)	c. 1639
Peter Davenport (1622-1658)	1655
William Davenport (7) (1643-1696)	1658
William Davenport (8) (1663-1706)	1696
John Davenport (3) (1695-1722)	1706
William Davenport (9) (1697-1729)	1722
Warren Davenport (1698-1749)	1729
William Davenport (10) (1745-1829)	1749

Salusbury (Pryce Humphreys) Davenport (1778-1845)	1829
Maria Davenport (1785-1866)	1845
William Davenport Davenport (1811-1869)	1854
John William Handley Davenport (1851-1914)	1869

Subsequent owners of Bramall Hall, with dates of ownership

The Freeholders Company Limited	1877-1883
Charles Henry Nevill (1848-1916)	1883-1916
Thomas Nevill Carleton Nevill (1879-1948)	1916-1925
John Henry Davies (1864-1927)	1925-1927
Amy Davies (1864-1937)	1927-1935
Hazel Grove & Bramhall Urban District Council	1935-1974
passing after local government reorganisation to	
Stockport Metropolitan Borough Council	1974-

INTRODUCTION

'For this house is one of the treasures of England.' So said Brigadier-General Sir William Bromley-Davenport, head of the Davenport family of Woodford and Capesthorne and Lord Lieutenant of Cheshire, when, on behalf of the Hazel Grove & Bramhall Urban District Council, he formally opened Bramall Hall to the public on Saturday, 18 April 1936.[1]

On this spring afternoon, in brilliant sunshine, the background of trees in the Park was just sufficiently green to provide a picturesque contrast with the black and white exterior of the Hall. A new Union Jack, floating where in former years the flag of the Davenports of Bramhall had flown, provided a vivid splash of colour. The invited guests first assembled in the courtyard; members and officials of the Hazel Grove & Bramhall Urban District Council with their families, visitors from neighbouring authorities and prominent citizens of the district, as well as three people who already loved the Hall as a home and represented by descent its former owners. Joan Davenport, a member of the family which had for so long held Bramhall, was great-granddaughter to Sir Salusbury and Lady Davenport who owned the estate in the early part of the nineteenth century. Captain T. N. C. Nevill inherited Bramall Hall from his uncle in 1916, and Elsie Partington was the daughter of John H. Davies, whose widow had recently sold the property to the Urban District Council.

Sir William, with his sister, Lady Ridley, were met at Bramall Hall gates by the Chairman of the Council, Leslie K. Gallaway, LL.B., and the Clerk of the Council, and escorted on foot up the drive. They made their way through the assembled guests and at the entrance to the building Sir William received from Mrs Elsie Partington the key to the west door. He unlocked the door and stepped through the small porch into the great hall. The guests followed slowly, in a long line, for the formal introductions which were to take place inside.

The proceedings which followed were conducted by Councillor Gallaway. The official party, with Sir William Bromley-Davenport and Lady Ridley, ranged themselves behind the massive oak refectory table which stands at the south end of the great hall. In addition to Frederick Capper, the Clerk of the Council, there were Herbert Johnson, a Bramhall councillor and Chairman of the newly-formed Parks & Estates Committee, and Joseph Gosling of the *Red Lion* hotel, Hazel Grove, the Vice-Chairman of the committee. To Leslie Gallaway, a Bramhall representative just completing his second consecutive year as Chairman of the Hazel Grove & Bramhall Urban District Council, the opening of Bramall Hall to the public came as the culminating event of two years of endeavour, and it was evident to all who heard him speak that he was captivated by the spirit of this historic building. 'It is to be maintained by the local authority in as nearly as possible the condition in which it has existed in the past', he said. 'We want it to be a place of historical, archæological and architectural research . . . We hope, above all, that the memories of the past associated with this old Hall will prove an inspiration to those who come after.'

The Hall was now bare and lacked furniture, explained Councillor Gallaway, and it was the policy of the Council that nothing should be introduced which was not in keeping with its ancient history. Councillor Johnson had already launched an appeal for appropriate furnishings, and already it was possible to see some valued gifts. The oak refectory table remained in the Hall through the generosity of Mrs Amy Davies (the last private owner) and a Jacobean oak chest with other pieces of period furniture came from Charles H. Wrigley. There were also three volumes of manuscript, compiled in the late-nineteenth century by a local antiquarian, Alfred Burton; these were the gift of Captain Nevill.

More was to come. The highlight of the afternoon came during the speech of the Lord Lieutenant. 'Others also have done their share and I should like to do mine', said Sir William. 'When you go through the Hall you will see the Paradise Room . . . It contained a four-poster bed profusely illustrated in needlework depicting the Garden of Eden and the fall of man. This needlework was the work of the lady of the house, Dame Dorothy Davenport, and she records that she was occupied for over thirty years in doing it . . . The bed is in my house at Capesthorne, and I should like to give it back. But I cannot give it back for it is not mine to give. When my father acquired it some years ago, for greater security he made it over as an heirloom to the trustees of the estate. But . . . I shall be glad to put it back in this room, with the undertaking that it shall not be moved from there in my lifetime.'

After the ceremony guests were conducted in small groups round the interior of the building, or they were free to wander in the grounds. The official opening had inaugurated a new era in the history of Bramall Hall. 'In generations to come', said Sir William Bromley-Davenport, 'this will be known as the day when Bramall Hall was saved.'

Chapter 1   THE GLORY OF BRAMALL HALL

'For charm of situation and picturesqueness in style of architecture, Bramall Hall is unrivalled amongst the many interesting "black and white" mansions of Cheshire' wrote an architect, Henry Taylor, in 1884. 'It stands in a delightfully undulating park, about two and a half miles south of Stockport, overlooking the Lyme Hills." The description is still recognisable today, although the face of the surrounding countryside, and to a certain extent the face of the Hall itself, is changed. The building is situated on high ground at the confluence of two streams, the Ladybrook (known in the seventeenth century as the River Brame) and its little tributary, the Carr Brook. Much of the black and white colouring still represents genuine half-timbered work of Tudor date, though repair and reconstruction have taken place over many years.

For hundreds of years the approach to Bramall Hall was from the eastern side by the carriage way leading from the Stockport road. The drive followed the course of the Ladybrook, then crossed the Carr Brook and, turning up the hill towards the chapel, it skirted the south wing of the Hall to reach the courtyard. Today the main entrance is on the west. From the courtyard on this side the method of construction of a Cheshire manor house can be clearly seen. The foundations were of stone, but the supports and crossbeams used for the main part of the building were of massive beams of oak. Whole tree trunks, smoothed and shaped with the adze and mortised and pegged together, gave the patterned outline of the building, the spaces in between being filled in with raddles and daub and covered with plaster. J. A. Gotch has vividly described the result.

> The contrast between the dark framework and the light-coloured plaster, together with the variety of line consequent upon the constructional necessities of the framework itself, insure a lively result; and when the straight lines of the greater part of the framing are relieved by the introduction of curved braces or more fanciful panels in the gables, the combination is very attractive. The effect is often enhanced by dainty little bits of detail in the wood finials and pendants and verge-boards, but even without these aids the texture of the wood becomes so beautiful

through age and weather as hardly to require the help of a chisel ...
There is a fine example at Bramall Hall, near Stockport.[2]

Not so much of the original work remains as when Gotch wrote, for
the north wing was in the mid-twentieth century extensively repaired on its
courtyard side, modern materials being used. The south wing, however,
and particularly the part immediately opposite the renovated north wing,
could be the earliest part of the present Hall. Beneath a small oriel window
projecting from the upper storey is a shield bearing one lion rampant, the
arms of de Bromale, the Norman family who held Bramhall until about
1370. After that date, when the estate passed by marriage to the Davenport
family, the arms of de Davenport — three cross croslets with a crescent for
difference — were quartered with those of de Bromale, and they are so
found in other parts of the building. The Bromale shield forms part of an
elaborately carved oak bracket on which the oriel window rests. The shield
is held by an angel figure with outstretched wings which looks down and
across the courtyard, and the whole design is resting on a man's head, out
of whose mouth come two long sprays of oak leaves. Is he the Green Man
or May King who, at mediaeval May Day festivals, heralded with his leafy
branches the new life of spring?

The Great Hall is entered from its north-west corner. Immediately
opposite is a heavy door in which there is a small wicket and which bears
much old metalwork; this was once the front entrance of Bramall Hall.
The passage formed through the great hall by the two doors seems to have
been responsible for the belief that there was a right of way through the
Hall. Harrison Ainsworth in the mid-nineteenth century helped to
popularise this idea. 'Such is Bramall', he wrote in his novel *Rookwood*,
describing in a digression the beauties of the black and white buildings of
Lancashire and Cheshire. 'As an illustration of old English hospitality ... it
may be mentioned, that a road conducted the passenger directly through
the great hall of this house, literally "of entertainment", where, if he listed,
strong ale, and other refreshments, awaited his acceptance and courted his
stay.'[3] The position of the buttery hatch, which communicated with the
kitchen through the screens and passage, can still be seen in the much-
restored north wall, and here, tradition claims, food would be handed out to
the poor of the district gathered outside the eastern entrance. There is,
however, no evidence of any right of way through Bramall Hall, and it is
probable that the main purpose of the small wicket within the larger door
was to restrain the stranger from entering before his credentials had been

checked. In order to pass through the small door it was necessary to lower the head and raise the knee — not an advantageous position for a potential enemy!

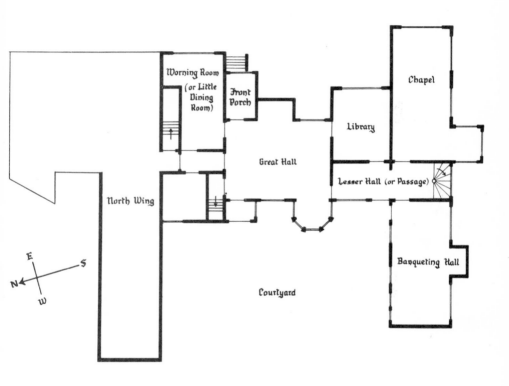

Bramall Hall : ground floor plan

The present great hall is probably a reconstruction of an older, single-storeyed building with open roof. The heavy timbers of the walls show clearly the marks of the adze, and one remaining pendant on the ceiling of

the bay indicates what the ceiling decoration of the whole room must once
have been like. The windows are mullioned and leaded and contain some
old shields of arms which commemorate alliances of the Davenport family
and of friendly families.[4] In the central light of the large bay window
overlooking the courtyard is the coat of arms of de Davenport quartering
that of de Bromale – a reminder of the Davenport-Bromale marriage – and
nearby are four roundels portraying Saturn, Mercury, Mars and Jupiter. A
long, narrow bench seat, probably of early-eighteenth-century date, is fixed
to the wall behind the refectory table; this south side of the hall was
originally reserved for the lord of the manor, his family and guests. The
large, open fireplace on the eastern side now has a heavy oak surround, and
shows the bear and ragged staff which the late-Victorian owner adopted as
his symbol.

The Library, on the south-east side of the great hall, has been much
modernised. The timbered ceiling has been decorated with cross work and
rose bosses almost certainly of nineteenth century date.

The Passage, or Lesser Hall, on the south-west side of the great hall,
is fully oak-panelled and the timbers of the ceiling are decorated as in the
library. Along the top of the panels an inscription is cut into the wood in
old English characters. The first two letters seem to have been reversed,
and it now reads:

IM	GH	T W	ITH	FOR	TIN	AND	GR	ACE	. . .

SO T	HAT	PRO	SEED	TO	VIR	TU	AND	GRA	CE

The window expanse of the great hall is continued along the west side of
the passage, and on one of the diamond-shaped panes is scratched the
signature 'S.P.Humphreys' – the signature of Captain (later Sir) Salusbury
Pryce Humphreys, husband of the heiress, Maria Davenport.,

A nineteenth-century archway leads to the rooms of the south wing,
with central staircase.

The Lower Banqueting Hall, on the west, presents a very solid
example of mediaeval carpentry. The heavy timbers of the ceiling and of
the north and east walls indicate the age of the room, and the large stone
bases on which they rest can be easily seen. The south and west walls have
at some time been cased in brick and plaster, and the south-east corner
shows signs of having been rebuilt and a doorway here closed. Traces of

coloured decoration, showing a type of geometrical pattern fashionable in the eighteenth century, still remain on the first two bays of the north wall, above the north door.

The Chapel, on the east, was for centuries the only place of public worship in Bramhall as well as being the domestic chapel of the Davenport family. At some time between 1869 and 1890 it was closed, and later completely dismantled. In 1938 it was faithfully restored to its old pattern, and religious services were resumed under the authority of the Hazel Grove & Bramhall Urban District Council. The services, which are now the responsibility of the Stockport Metropolitan Borough Council, are freely open to all and are conducted in turn by the various clergy and ministers in the area, according to their particular pattern of Christian worship.

In the north wall of the chapel are mullioned windows, with arched tracery. These windows have never been glazed and they now look on to the wall of the library, with only a few inches space between. Their origin is obscure, but they do provide some evidence that the south wing was once a separate building from the great hall. The low, flat ceiling timbers are of great age and on the upper and lower timbers of the west wall can be found corresponding Roman numerals — typical marks of the mediaeval carpenter, showing him where he should slot and peg the beams.

High on the west wall are painted the Ten Commandments in gothic black letter. Much of the lettering has flaked away — particularly from the portions painted over the timber — and there has been clearly revealed part of an older painting. On the centre beam can be seen the upper part of a figure of Christ, the head crowned with thorns, a cross supported below, and in a band on the right-hand side the word *HOMO*. Here, it would seem, there was once a Passion painting with the inscription *ECCE HOMO* ('Behold the man'). The picture was overpainted with the Commandments, probably in the reign of Queen Elizabeth I, but now, after some four hundred years, it has revealed itself again.

The oldest item of furniture in the chapel is a box pew which is believed to have come from the Davenport chapel in Stockport Parish Church. The stall has a fine example of a poppy head, and the woodcarving on the side of the pew shows the arms of Davenport of Bramhall (three cross croslets with a crescent for difference) with on either side a lion passant and various grotesque creatures. Above the shield of the Davenports is the badge of the house of Plantagenet — the rose and the fetterlock surmounted by the crown — which would date the pew as not later than the time of Richard III.

The Ball Room, or Upper Banqueting Room, on the first floor, has an arched roof with carved timbers. The central window on the north side is that little oriel, projecting into the courtyard, under which is carved the de Bromale shield. The most striking feature of the room is the wonderful mural decoration on the north and east walls, in which various strange scenes are depicted. On the north wall, for instance, there is the boy on horseback, tilting at a windmill, but the horse has the head of a cock. This might be a representation of the old nursery rhyme 'Ride a cock horse' or it could be intended to depict the very popular scene from Cervantes' *Don Quixote* which had been published in English in 1612. Among the pictures on the east wall, where once may have been a musicians' gallery, there is the clearly defined figure of a man with a mandoline. He is playing from a scroll of music held by a lady who wears a long gown and a cap with lapels. These murals, and the lettering round the upper parts of the walls, are probably of late-sixteenth- or early-seventeenth-century date.

The Chapel Room, or Queen Anne Room, is in its present form almost entirely the work of the late-nineteenth-century restorer. In later Davenport days the room had been divided into two, probably by a light partition wall, the first part being known as the 'ante-room' and the larger part as the 'state bedroom'. This room has also gained the name of the 'priest's room', and, being over the chapel, it would be the most likely room to be given for the priest's use, were there ever a priest resident in Bramall Hall. Hidden behind the oak panelling on the north side of the room is an ancient doorway which has been filled in with wattle and daub. It appears much too old in date to have anything to do with a priest's hide, and is more likely to be part of the original structure of the chapel wing. Despite all conjecture as to where the door led, its real purpose remains a mystery.

The Plaster Room, so called because at one time it had a plaster floor, occupies the space between the chapel room and the withdrawing room, but is on a lower level than either. On the north wall are the initials of William and Dorothy Davenport (who reconstructed Bramall Hall) and the date 1599.

The Paradise Room opens off the plaster room on its eastern side. The name was often used, in the Middle Ages, for a bedroom or favourite apartment, but at Bramall Hall it has special significance because of the 'Paradise Bed' which for so long stood here.

The floor of the room is of solid oak and the walls are panelled nearly to the ceiling, with a plaster frieze of ornamental fruit and foliage. Two windows give a view eastwards towards the Derbyshire hills. There is a fireplace in the south wall and behind the panelling on the window side is a large cavity, until recently hidden by modern boarding. On the other side of the fireplace is a cupboard, probably replacing an older closet built in a deep recess. These recesses were mentioned in a description of 1882 before the Victorian alterations:

> A small closet occupies the space on one side the fireplace, and on the corresponding side there is a dark passage which is said to lead to some region unknown.[5]

Here – near to the chapel and the chapel room, within the family apartments and away from the prying eyes of servants – is the most likely place in Bramall Hall to find a priest's hide. Such a hide could have been built into the wall in the thickness of the old chimney breast between the paradise room and the chapel room. It could have been constructed about 1580, near the height of the religious persecution of Elizabeth I's reign, when the mistress of the house was a known recusant. By the nineteenth century the paradise room had earned the alternative name of the 'ghost room' and legends of hauntings had grown up around it.

> And rustling garments oft are heard,
> And sounds that oft appall,

wrote a collector of Cheshire legends when putting into verse a tale of Bramall Hall which he had heard from its mid-nineteenth-century owner.[6] There are also stories of a secret way leading from the paradise room to the drive outside or down to the chapel, and of possibilities of escape towards Stockport by this route, but these are imaginative tales only. It has been suggested that such legends often cling to a place which harbours a secret room or priest's hide, and may even have been fostered by the desire to cover up the strange comings and goings there.[7]

The Withdrawing Room – the finest room in the house – occupies the whole of the space above the great hall. The large expanse of glass facing the courtyard is even more extensive than in the room below, and, to the right of the fireplace, on the opposite wall, is an oriel window giving a view to the east. A handsome plaster overmantel above the fireplace reaches to the ceiling, as was fashionable in Tudor times. It bears the arms of Queen Elizabeth I, supported on the one side by the lion rampant and on the other by the dragon. Tradition has it that the overmantel was presented by the Queen herself on one of her 'progresses' as a thank-offering for hospitality received, but there is not the slightest evidence for this. On the contrary, the Queen never seems to have come even as far north as Chester.

Nevertheless the provision of such a magnificent overmantel in this beautiful new room of their house does indicate the intense loyalty of its designers to their sovereign. The ceiling, too, is of plaster, highly ornamented and with hanging pendants each of individual design, and on a plaster frieze above the wall panelling are fifteen shields of arms commemorating marriages of the Davenport family. Much of the decorative work on the north door is of Italian design, with some fine inlay work, and above the lintel on the left side is the pentacle, or five-pointed star formed in an endless knot, which was often used above doorways and thresholds as a charm to repel evil spirits.

The Davenport Bedroom, which is in the northernmost part of the main block, is fully panelled and has two smaller rooms leading from it. On the south side is a dressing room and on the north a closet, built in a narrow passage between this bedroom and the next. The closet has been much altered, but it is possible that it once concealed a second secret room, built either as an alternative hide for a priest or as a place of refuge for a Royalist during the Civil War.

The North Wing provided further bedroom accommodation above the servants' hall and working quarters downstairs. 'These rooms are mostly small, badly lighted, and ill arranged', wrote J. P. Earwaker in 1877.[8] In fact, they have been so remodelled over the years in order to provide the appurtenances considered necessary in each generation for a great house, that little of antiquity now remains. Even so, some roof timbers indicate that, in origin, this wing is at least as old as the rest of the building.

The present Bramall Hall – even the oldest parts of it – cannot have formed part of the original dwelling of the family which made this district their own. Local legend gives the site of the first hall of the Bromales as Crow Holt Wood, a half-mile to the south, where still remain artificial ditches which were thought to have formed part of a moat. In his manuscript *History of Bramhall* Alfred Burton, the late-nineteenth-century antiquarian, plotted a diagram of these earthworks as they remained in 1880, and wrote:

> On the summit of the rising ground to the south of the hall, (and which is the highest ground in the township, affording a fine view of the surrounding country,) are the remains of the first hall erected by the Bromhales. The spot is now covered with a fine plantation, and is known as 'Fairy Wood', the legend being that as fast as the builders laid the stones and timbers in the daytime the fairies removed them in the night to the present spot, till the owner, tired of his fruitless struggle, abandoned the spot and erected the hall in its present position. [1]

Burton was obviously convinced that a hall once stood in Crow Holt Wood. Tradition claimed that Bramhall was crossed by roads of Roman origin; the one – marked as Roman on the first six-inch ordnance survey maps – coming from Stockport (a minor Roman station) and following the route of the present Bramhall Lane; the other entering Bramhall from Cheadle by Ack Lane, meeting the first at or near Lumb Lane and continuing south-east through Adlington. Burton saw the Crow Holt Wood site as having the advantages of high ground for defence and the amenities of the equidistant Roman roads for travel.

An alternative and more likely explanation of the structure in 'Fairy Wood' was given in 1909 by Frederick Moorhouse who came to the conclusion that it had once been an old deerhay into which periodically deer could be driven for sorting and taking alive. Local residents still insisted that Bramall Hall should have been built there, but that the site was abandoned in favour of the present position. This explanation Moorhouse could not accept. Careful investigation convinced him that the tradition was very shadowy, and the site of the present hall much better, especially for defence and because of its proximity to the little River Brame. He found

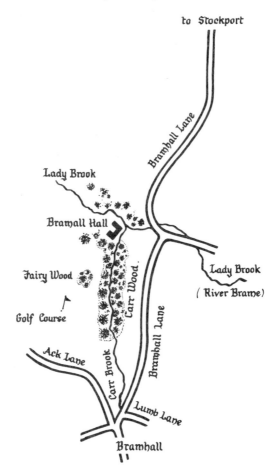

Site of Bramall Hall in relation to main roads and streams

that the earthworks consisted of two hollow enclosures, divided by, and surrounded by, ramparts, with a narrow opening through which, according to his theory, the deer would be driven. 'The reason for the double compartment', he said, 'was that by manipulation of the gates they could separate cattle from deer or stags from does, etc., and as one of the classes would always be larger than the other the compartments or enclosures were adapted accordingly.'[2] When Frederick Moorhouse examined the remains of the deerhay – if such it is – it was surrounded by thick copse and situated on still undeveloped land belonging to the Freeholders Company. Today it remains, shorn of most of its former glory, a landmark near the footpath across the Bramhall Park golf links.

Perhaps this old earthwork was the 'haia' or 'half a hay' – the hay in process of construction – of Domesday Bramhall. Perhaps, too, the three-quarter-mile length of Carr Wood nearby is all that remains of the wood 'half a league long and the same broad' mentioned in that same Domesday survey. If so, these are relics of Hamon, the first Norman holder of the manor of Bramhall. Here is the Domesday entry for Bramhall:

> The same Hamon holds BRAMALE. Brun and Hacun held (it) as 2 manors, and were free men. There is 1 hide that pays geld. There is land (enough) for 6 ploughs. One radman and 2 villeins and 2 bordars have 1 plough there. There is wood(land) half a league long and as much wide, and half a hay, and an acre of meadow. It was worth 32 shillings T.R.E.; now 5 shillings. He found it waste.[3]

Before the Norman Conquest there was obviously a Saxon settlement here, but whether the Saxon landowners, Brun and Hacun, both held manors in the place now known as Bramhall or whether one belonged to a place unspecified in the record, it is impossible to say. And was Brun, who held a manor in Bramhall, the same Brun who also held Aldrelie (Over Alderley), Nordberie (Norbury) and Caleford (Chelford)? Certainly Hamon, who after the Norman Conquest became Baron of Dunham Massey, was one of the most powerful men in Cheshire. He is listed in the Domesday Book as owning seven manors (Bramhall in Macclesfield hundred, Dunham, Bowdon, Hale, Ashley and Ollerton in Bucklow hundred, and Puddington in Wirral) and he also held other lands jointly around Altrincham and Baguley and in Eastham on the Wirral.

In Bramhall Hamon had six ploughlands which could represent about 720 acres under cultivation, or suitable for cultivation, though only one plough team was working there. The duty of the radman would be to carry on the work of the holding; there were also two villeins who were virtually serfs, and two bordars, or peasants, who might hold cottages or land, and would farm for their lord. Even when allowance is made for the families of the people mentioned in the survey, the sparseness of the population at this time is obvious.

The Domesday record for Bramhall supplies value figures for the land at three different dates, and from these figures an interesting comparison can be made.

It was worth 32 shillings **T.R.E.; now** 5 shillings. **He found it** waste.

When Hamon de Massy ('he') acquired the manor in or about the year 1070, it was 'waste', probably having been completely devastated by the Norman army during William the Conqueror's harsh subdual of Cheshire. By 1086 ('now' – the date of the survey) some of the land was under cultivation again, but recovery must have come about only slowly. The land value was still less than one-sixth of its pre-1066 figure ('Tempus Regis Edwardi' – the time of King Edward, the Confessor), when there could have been a moderately prosperous settlement here.

The Domesday spelling of 'Bramale' is the earliest form of the name known and indicates the Saxon origin of the place. The word is derived from the Old English *brom*, meaning broom, and *halh*, a nook or secret place, probably by the water. Bramhall must once have been 'a broomy nook' near the waters. The family who, in the early years of Norman rule, made this district their home, took their name from the place; they did not give a name to the place. The founder of the de Bromale family was probably a follower or relative of that Hamon de Massy mentioned in the Domesday Book, and he presumably received his lands in Bramhall as a reward for services rendered.

In the time of Henry II a certain Matthew de Bromale received a confirmation of his lands in Bramhall from Hamon, the second Baron of Dunham Massey, who released him from all services previously rendered 'except the service of the fee of one breastplate'.[4] Matthew's father is stated to have held these lands previously; he may have been the kinsman of the first Hamon de Massy. Matthew was succeeded by his grandson, Richard, who accumulated further power to himself when he obtained a grant that his tenants need no longer be tried in the Baron's court in Dunham, but locally in Bramhall. Two more Richards succeeded in the direct line, the last of that name dying without issue. This Richard was succeeded by his younger brother, Geoffrey, who had two daughters, Alice and Ellen. Alice, who about 1370 or 1380 married John de Davenport of Wheltrough, inherited the Bramhall lands and became the ancestress of the Davenport family of Bramhall. It could have been about this time that the earliest parts of the Bramall Hall we now know were being built.

Chapter 3   DAVENPORT OF BRAMHALL – 400 years of male
                                                 succession

The early Davenports

The Davenport family of Cheshire traces its descent from Orm de
Davenport who was living during, or just after, the time of William the
Conqueror, and who probably took his name from 'Dauen-port', the 'town
on the trickling stream' where he lived. Davenport, on the River Dane, is a
few miles north-west of Congleton and not far from the village of Marton
where the Davenport family soon became important landowners. In the
early-thirteenth century the office of grand serjeant of the forest of
Macclesfield was granted to Vivian Davenport, the head of the family, and
it is to this office, which became hereditary, that the Davenports have
always attributed the felon's head crest which surmounts their shield of
arms. This 'man's head couped at the shoulders proper, around the neck a
rope or' is said to signify the absolute powers of life and death which the
grand serjeant held within the forest, and his duty to search out and hang
the robbers lurking within its boundaries. Other suggestions contained in
story and legend are not so kind to the Davenports and offer less worthy
reasons for the adoption of this sinister-looking badge.[1] Sufficient to say
that the crest became common to all branches of the Davenport family in
Cheshire and representations of it can still be seen in and around
Capesthorne Hall, on the painted inn sign of the *Davenport Arms* at
Woodford, and at Bramall Hall. Here, in Davenport days, two great
heads of stone, each bearing a halter around its neck, surmounted the
gateposts at the southern end of the drive, loftily surveying all comers and
claiming family ownership for the grounds.

During the fourteenth century branches of the Davenport family
became established at Wheltrough, at Henbury, at Woodford, and finally –
by the marriage of John de Davenport and Alice de Bromale – at Bramhall.
From about 1400 to 1829 Davenport followed Davenport in strict
succession, the Bramhall family being fortunate during these four centuries
in always having a male heir to succeed.

Robert, the son of John and Alice, was the first real Davenport of Bramhall, and when in 1397 he married Joan de Assheton an elaborate financial agreement provided for part of her dowry to be returned should either party die within three years of marriage. The arrangements proved unnecessary, for Robert and Joan were married for forty years and they had four children. Their eldest son, who died before his father, married a daughter of the Fitton family of Gawsworth, and their grandson, John (the heir), was the first member of the Davenport family to marry a Warren of Poynton. His marriage to Cicely Warren in 1435 forged a link with that family which was to become even stronger in Elizabethan times and, again, at the beginning of the eighteenth century.

John de Davenport was lord of the manor from 1436 to 1478 and during the latter part of this period the Wars of the Roses were taking their toll in Lancashire and Cheshire. Most of the local families were involved on one side or the other and change of allegiance among the leaders was by no means unknown. Not until seven years after John's death did the Wars come to an end, and then his son and heir, William, was probably on the winning side.

It is interesting to note the consequences of the alliance which John de Davenport arranged for his daughter, Margaret. When, in 1460, Margaret, of Bramhall, married Nicholas Davenport of Woodford, these two branches of the Davenport family became doubly united. From the Davenports of Woodford the present Bromley-Davenport family has descent. They, like the Davenports of Bramhall, can claim as ancestor, Alice de Bromale, as well as (two hundred years earlier) Orm de Davenport.

Tudor and early Stuart Davenports

1478–1528	The first William Davenport
1528–1541	The second William Davenport
1541–1576	The third William Davenport
1576–1585	The fourth William Davenport
1585–1639	The fifth William Davenport

William Davenport – the first of that name – was lord of the manor of Bramhall for fifty years, and he lived to be eighty-two years old. Presumably he took an active part in the Battle of Bosworth which, in 1485, ended the Wars of the Roses and put Henry VII on the throne of

England. Under the leadership of Lord Stanley (successor to the Masseys as the overlord of the Davenports) many Cheshire men marched to the support of Henry Tudor. The following year, when Stanley had been created the first Earl of Derby by the new king, William Davenport was granted an annuity of 20 marks a year for life, and this could have been in recognition of his services on the battlefield.[2]

About ten years later William Davenport's house – or one of his houses – seems to have been one of nine houses destroyed by Randle Hassall, who carried off the timber, and for whose arrest a warrant was issued.[3] Was it Bramall Hall that was destroyed – or, perhaps, partially destroyed? If so, there is support for Alfred Burton's theory that the south end of the great hall was rebuilt during the reign of Henry VII, the present library and lesser hall being formed from part of it.

The first William Davenport is chiefly notable now as one of the original trustees of the Macclesfield Grammar School (known today as *The King's School*) which was founded in 1502 under the will of Sir John Percyvale. It was to be 'a Free Grammar School, teaching there gentlemen's sons and other good men's sons of the town and country thereabouts'. This was just fifty years before the school received its royal charter from Edward VI, giving it a 'License by Letters Patent for the education of boys in grammatical learning and good manners'.

The second William Davenport was a younger son of the first, and already a middle-aged man when he succeeded his father. It would probably be during the time of his lordship that John Leland, chaplain, librarian and antiquary to King Henry VIII, passed through Bramhall on his travels, and recorded in his *Itinerary*:

> Davenport of Bromehaule 2 miles from Stopporde by West dwellith at Bromehaule. He hath a 2. markes landes.[4]

It is not, however, for his life, but in his death, that this William Davenport is now memorable, for his will, dated 1 June 1541, has been preserved and published.[5] It is of special interest and importance in the history of Bramall Hall chapel.

> I will that myne executo[rs] cause an honest priest to celebrate masse and other devine service for the soulles of me my father my mother my aunceto[rs] and all Christen soulles in the church of Stopford and chappell of Bromall by the space of one wholle yeare next after my deathe ffor convenient wage so to do . . .

Here is the first known record of the existence of a chapel at Bramall Hall. There is no doubt about the sacred nature of this building, in which religious services were held as early as 1541 and where the impact of the English Reformation had not yet been felt.

Instructions as to his burial were given in William Davenport's will. 'I bequeth . . . my bodie to be buryed in the chappell of o^r blessed Lady wth in the churche of Stopforde apon the southe syde of the same chappell where my anncesto^{rs} be buryed.' This south chantry chapel in the old Stockport Parish Church was shared by two families, the Davenports of Bramhall and the Arderns of Hardern. The Davenports took the southern side, and it is clear that there was an altar here, where a priest, paid by the Davenport family, regularly offered mass. In this chapel generations of future Davenports were also to be buried.

An inventory of the goods and chattels of William Davenport, made after his death later in the year 1541, lists the number and value of his farm stock and shows him to be a wealthy man, putting out sheep to graze in Derbyshire as well as in Cheshire. The furnishings of his 'chambers' are described room by room, and a 'yate house chamber' is mentioned, showing that at this date there was a fourth side to the hall, with an entrance by a gatehouse. Mention is also made of the 'chapell chamber' – the room above the chapel – which may also have been the priest's room.

The third William Davenport was twenty years old and already married with young children when he succeeded to the estate. In 1544, when he was twenty-three, he took part in a punitive expedition against the Scots, ordered by Henry VIII after the Scots had repudiated the agreement for the betrothal of their infant queen, Mary, to the King's son, Edward. The English force under the Earl of Hertford (later Duke of Somerset) was sent to lay waste the land between Berwick and Edinburgh, to take Edinburgh and to burn the town. For his part in the affair – whatever this may have been – William Davenport was knighted by the Earl. The honour was not unique, for, after the sacking of Edinburgh, Hertford honoured nearly sixty squires in this way, one third of them being Cheshire men.[6]

Sir William Davenport, in his thirty-five years' lordship at Bramhall, successfully survived the most violent period of religious upheaval that England has known. Born and brought up in the early days of the English Reformation, he was to see an extreme form of Protestantism established under Edward VI and then violently overthrown by the Roman Catholic

Queen Mary. He was to live through the first eighteen years of Queen Elizabeth I and to see the gradual emergence of the Church of England as a real and stable institution. Through all these changes we can only guess that his life was centred in his home and manor, and that the honour of his family meant more to him than political and religious change.

This view is confirmed by the fact that it must have been this William Davenport who was the originator of the Bramhall heraldic tapestry. His second marriage, about 1560, to Anna Brereton of Tatton, is the latest marriage commemorated on the tapestry, and the shield portraying it occupies the central position in the line of shields along one of the long borders. Near to it are shields commemorating the marriages of his two daughters by his first wife, and his own marriage to Margaret Booth, their mother. Further shields on this same border are those of his ancestors and of his son, William. Shields of friendly families are continued in a successive line around the remaining three borders, this arrangement making it appear as though the tapestry were intended as a cover, perhaps for the high table. A large Tudor shield occupies the centre of the tapestry, flanked on the left by the shield of the fifth Earl of Shrewsbury and on the right by that of the third Earl of Derby, each shield being surrounded by the Garter. The Tudor shield could be that of Queen Mary or Queen Elizabeth, but even if the work was begun in the reign of Mary (who died in 1558) it must have been finished in the reign of Elizabeth I.

In the lives of his daughters Sir William Davenport saw both godliness and tragedy. His elder daughter, Elizabeth, was married to the young Richard Ashton, son and heir of Richard Ashton of Middleton. He died in 1563, and in the early years of her widowhood Elizabeth came under conviction for felony and murder, remaining so until the day of her death.[7] Her lands were deemed forfeit to the Crown; first to Queen Elizabeth and later to King James I. She lived to be nearly seventy, and died disgraced. By contrast, the younger daughter, Katherine, died in her father's lifetime, having acquired a reputation for goodness hard to equal. She had married, about 1560, Sir Richard Bulkeley of Beaumaris and Cheadle, and after her death in 1573 an Anglesey poet wrote 'An Epitaphe upon the Deathe: of the Right Worshipfull Mystres Katheryne Bulkley . . .'

> She was a perfect Jem of Joye, a Lampe of godlye Light,
> A myrroure for benignytie: a famous worthye wight.
> A matron mother to the poore: and frend unto the rest,
> An enemye to no Degree: a patterne to the best.

After extolling her many virtues, the poet concluded his lines:

> By hope we may assure our selves, her state thryse happie is,
> Her cares quyte changed unto Joye, and to eternall blisse. [8]

The son and heir of Sir William Davenport – himself another William Davenport – succeeded his father in 1576 and was lord of the manor for nine years. These years were some of the most crucial in the religious struggle of Elizabeth I's reign; years of fierce persecution for Catholics, but years when their zeal for the reconversion of England was at its height, and when Catholic priests, specially trained in seminaries abroad, were sent to England in secret for this purpose. This is the time for a priest's hide in Bramall Hall to have been built, and it would be built under this William Davenport's instructions. His wife, Margaret (the daughter of Richard Ashton of Middleton) was a convinced Catholic, and perhaps William Davenport himself would have been, had not the pull towards conformity been so great.

On 15 October 1581 two of William Davenport's children were married at Prestbury Parish Church to children of John and Margaret Warren of Poynton. William, the heir to the Bramhall estate, married Dorothy Warren (these two were later to become Sir William and Dame Dorothy, of Bramall Hall fame), and Anne Davenport, William's only sister, was married to Dorothy's brother, Edward. Two years later, State Papers of Queen Elizabeth gave the names of twelve gentlemen and one lady in Cheshire 'whose houses are greatlie infected with popery, and not loked unto'. Among the names was that of William Davenport of Bramhall, who, with his wife, 'never cometh at Churche, and his famyly are greatly infected'. [9] It then appeared that William Davenport, his wife and family, had discreetly withdrawn to Westmorland, probably to Margaret's mother's home, for she was of the family of Bellingham of Burnside.

In 1585 the fourth William Davenport died and during the next few years his widow seems to have suffered, first, from the heavy fines which the act against recusancy imposed and, later, from seizure of her dower lands. Within her family there must have been deep religious division. Her eldest son, William, and her illustrious lawyer-son, Humphrey (he who was later Lord Chief Baron of the Exchequer and was called upon to pronounce the majority verdict in the Ship Money trial of John Hampden), prospered within the framework of Elizabethan and Anglican society, but at least one of Margaret's other sons entered the seminary at Valladolid in

Spain, and became a Roman Catholic priest.

The fifth William Davenport was almost eighteen years of age when he married Dorothy Warren at Prestbury and twenty-two when he inherited the manor of Bramhall. For nearly fifty-five years Sir William and Dame Dorothy (as they became) lived at Bramall Hall, enlarging and beautifying the building as was fashionable in the late-Elizabethan and the Jacobean age.

William and Dorothy had eleven children. Child betrothals were still customary in the landed families, and there is an example of an actual child marriage in the Davenport family at this time. On 25 June 1599 Penelope, the fourth daughter of William and Dorothy Davenport, was married at Prestbury to Jasper Worth, of Titherington, 'both being very young'.[10] Penelope was, in fact, five years old. The first marriage recorded as 'at Bramhall' is that of William, eldest son of William and Dorothy, who on 30 October 1599 married Frances Wilbraham, of Woodhey. William, the son, was then fifteen years old, and his bride, eleven. Bramall Hall chapel was evidently by now licensed for weddings, though the entry of the marriage was made in the register at Stockport Parish Church.

The fifth William Davenport was knighted by King James I, probably on 22 April 1603 at Newark-on-Trent where the King stayed overnight on his six weeks' journey from Edinburgh to London to claim the English throne.[11] Queen Elizabeth had died on 24 March 1603 and her successor, James VI of Scotland, who became James I of England, made a leisurely journey to the English capital, receiving the homage of his new subjects on the way and scattering his favours with a liberal hand. William Davenport of Bramhall was only one of over two hundred persons on whom knighthood was bestowed during the first six weeks of the new reign.

In 1604 Sir William Davenport served as High Sheriff of Cheshire, and in 1610 he was one of four commissioners for the hundred of Macclesfield appointed to assess and collect a subsidy levied for the Crown on landowners within the hundred. As lord of the manor of Bramhall he had his court leet and court baron, where tenants were tried by a jury of their peers, personal actions were decided, and necessary work on the maintenance of hedges, highways, and bridges within the township was enforced. There still remain some records of actions brought to the court both in Sir William Davenport's time and that of his immediate successors.[12]

To judge by the dates which they have left as record, Sir William and Dame Dorothy must have spent some twenty years in the reconstruction and decoration of Bramall Hall. Above the north door of the withdrawing room a piece of wood carving bore the date 1592, and on the north wall of the plaster room are the initials W D D and the date 1599. The overmantel in the withdrawing room must have been in place by 1603, the year in which Queen Elizabeth I died for, besides the wording 'Vive la Royne' there is a golden dragon used as one of the supporters of the royal shield. James I, who was a Scotsman, substituted the unicorn for the Welsh dragon. A carved Davenport family shield over the fireplace in the great hall had as inscription 'Sir William Davenport; Dame Dorothy Davenport; 1609', and the decorations of the roof timbers in the open roof above the chapel room bore the signature 'W D K [William Davenport, knight] 1610'. During these years the great hall must have been largely rebuilt and the withdrawing room constructed above it. A long gallery – that most typical and striking feature of the Elizabethan manor house – was later added as a third storey. There must have been extensive internal decoration to the rooms of the south wing, as indicated by the paintings on the roof of the chapel room and the walls of the upper banqueting room. Much of the decoration in this room is typical 'antique work' in tempera, giving an imitation tapestry effect very popular at the end of the sixteenth century.

It is reasonable to suppose that the lettering of the Ten Commandments on the west wall of Bramall Hall chapel was done in the time of Sir William and Dame Dorothy. Passion pictures were not officially permitted during the reign of Elizabeth I because they smacked of Roman Catholicism, but the Queen's tastes were quite opposed to the starkness of extreme Protestantism. Her direction that there should be set up in every church 'tables of the Decalogue' was intended to serve for the beautifying of the building and a reminder that it was a place of prayer. The instruction, given in 1561, was only slowly acted upon, and it is highly improbable that Sir William Davenport's predecessors – especially his Roman Catholic mother, Margaret – would wish to comply with it. The over-painting of the Passion picture would be delayed until at least 1585 and can be considered as part of Sir William and Dame Dorothy Davenport's redecoration of Bramall Hall.

A collection of family portraits was now being built up by the Davenports, as was becoming fashionable in late-Tudor and Stuart times. The earliest known are pictures of Dame Dorothy's parents, John and Margaret Warren, dated 1580 and 1595 respectively, and of her brother,

Sir Edward Warren, dated 1594. These portraits are painted directly on to wood, and John Warren and his son are shown wearing gold chains around their necks, as was customary for gentlemen of their time. A portrait of Henry, fourth Earl of Derby, painted in 1583, indicates the close connection between the Davenports of Bramhall and the Stanley family. Next in time is the portrait of Frances Davenport (née Wilbraham), child-wife of the eldest son of William and Dorothy. It was painted in 1602 when Frances was fourteen years of age, and the young girl wears a white satin bridal dress. Frances lived until about 1626 and bore her husband eight children. The line of Davenport was continued through her, although she never lived to be mistress of Bramall Hall.

The portraits of the lord and lady of the house were painted in 1627, when Sir William was aged 65 and his wife 66. The following year, 1628, there appeared a double portrait of their eldest son, William, holding the hand of his second wife, Margaret (née Legh), whom he had married only a few months earlier. William and Margaret were both aged 44.

A final treasure which survives from these years was the work of Dame Dorothy Davenport alone. The lovely piece of needlework, worked on worsted for her Paradise Bed, must have occupied Dame Dorothy for many of the later years of her life. For the head of the bed she worked, in three sections of needlework, the story of the Garden of Eden and Man's fall from Paradise. Eve is seen offering the apple to Adam, and coiled round the tree is the serpent. Then follows the Judgment scene, with the subsequent expulsion from the Garden, the Angel with the flaming sword being seen in the foliage of the tree. Finally, Adam and Eve are shown at their work, Adam with his spade and Eve with her spindle. Man's toil on earth has now begun.

For the top of the bed, Dame Dorothy embroidered a canopy with a pattern of flowers and leaves, and round the canopy she worked the following lines:

> Feare god and sleepe in peace: That thou in chryste mayste reste:. To passe theis dayes of sinne: And raigne with him in blisse: Where angells do remayne: And blesse and praise his name: With songes of Joy and happines: And live with him for ever: Therefore o lord in thee: Is my full hope and truste: That thou wilt mee defend: From sinne the worlld and Divel: Who goeth about to catch: Poore sinners in their snare: And bringe them to that place: Where.greefe and sorrowes are: Soe now I end my lynes: And worke that hath beene longe: To those that do them reade: In hope they will be pleasd **ʒ** by me: Dorithy Davenporte ·:1636:·

At the foot of the bed she worked on the canopy the initials and dates:
W D at one end, and D D at the other end.
1610   1614

Dame Dorothy died in November 1639, three years after she had
finished this work, aged seventy-seven. Sir William probably predeceased
her by a few months. They were spared seeing their country — peaceful and
prosperous for so many years — in the grip of civil war.

Civil War, Commonwealth and later Stuart Davenports

1639–1655   The sixth William Davenport
1655–1658   Peter Davenport
1658–1696   The seventh William Davenport
1696–1706   The eighth William Davenport

The sixth William Davenport was fifty-five years old when he
succeeded his father and he had a grown-up family by his first wife and
step-children by his second. On the day that he had married Margaret (née
Legh) the widow of Henry Arderne, Margaret's daughter Frances had been
married to William's eldest son (another William) thus seemingly securing
the family descent through Margaret. This was not to be, for the young
William died without issue at the beginning of 1642 and the second son,
Peter, became his father's heir. In September of that same year the Civil
War broke out, and it had immediate repercussions on the life of William
Davenport.

The county families of Cheshire were divided in their sympathies, but
those who favoured Parliament were much the more influential and
dedicated to their cause than those who favoured the King. William
Davenport was a Royalist by conviction and temperament, but his
allegiance seems to have been somewhat half-hearted. He left a Diary
giving a record of his sufferings and, as he saw them, undeserved
humiliations, during the years of the Civil War. Substantial extracts from
the Diary, together with a letter written by William Davenport's tenants on
the outbreak of war, have been published;[13] they give a clear picture of his
woes — caught as he was between the two opposing parties — during the
next three years.

The letter gave William Davenport an ultimatum. His tenants assured
him that they had 'these manie dayes with sadd spiritts weighed not onelie
the wofull distractions off our kingdome but also the present standinge that

is betwixt your Wors^{pe} and ourselves'. They had decided, 'wee dare not lifte upp our handes against that honorable assembly off Parlament'; they were unwilling to venture their lives 'in causes that our harts and consciences doe perswade us are not good or laweffull'. Without waiting for an answer, the signatories to the letter, with some of William Davenport's other tenants, enlisted the very next day as soldiers of the Parliament.

Then began a period of continual disturbance for William Davenport of Bramhall. Troops of first one side and then the other arrived at the Hall for quartering, and they took away horses and household goods and provisions. One morning in the spring of 1643 Sir William Brereton, commander-in-chief of the Parliamentary forces in Cheshire, himself arrived. He took away all the arms he could find, including a lance horseman's outfit which William Davenport valued at £40, but he promised Mr and Mrs Davenport that, as he had now disarmed them, he would defend them from the Parliamentary party. Ever since that time, according to William Davenport in 'A Briefe Summary of my sufferinges in some speciall passages' he and his wife had paid all taxes demanded of them, given quarter and entertainment to Parliamentary soldiers, sustained many losses and indignities by their own tenants and others, and never opposed the Parliamentary party.

Late in 1643 William Davenport's gray nag and his 'son Arderens' mare were stolen from the Park by four soldiers from the Parliamentary headquarters at Nantwich. The 'son' mentioned here would be William Davenport's stepson. Mr Arderne's horse was later recovered, but Mr Davenport's 'could never be had'.

On New Year's Day, 1644, Sir William Brereton with some of his officers and men again visited Bramhall, taking horses from stable and Park and removing Mr Davenport's fowling piece and various other items from the house. Mrs Davenport must have remonstrated with them, and had a promise that the things would be returned. Most never came back, and, of the horses which were returned, William Davenport reports rather gloomily that his young horse 'dyed within a while after'.

On Monday, 20 May 1644, William Davenport was at Woodford with his 'cosen Davenport' when a certain Robert Norbury, with other soldiers of the Parliament, forcibly took his mare from him, obliging him to return home on foot. Two days later soldiers from the same troop arrived for quartering in Bramhall, and the day after that Robert Norbury himself appeared, riding on Davenport's saddle but not on his mare. Norbury refused to restore the mare until he had received his Captain Stanley's permission, and that night soldiers of the Parliament were again quartered in Bramhall. At the week-end one of the main lines of battle passed right through Bramhall. On the Saturday Prince Rupert, with Royalist forces of the north and west, arrived in Cheadle and the Parliamentary forces melted away. At Stockport, too, the Parliamentary forces dispersed, and the Prince took the town with barely a struggle. The next day Royalist officers and their men were quartered in Bramall Hall; when they left William Davenport found he had lost three horses. Prince Rupert pushed on towards Bolton and Liverpool, but immediately came Lord Goring at the head of a large contingent of Royalist cavalry requiring quarters between Lyme and Stockport. William Davenport accommodated several officers, their men and their horses, at Bramhall; on their departure he lost three more horses. The final insult came a fortnight later when Parliamentary soldiers returned to Bramhall. They took away all the horses they could find in the Park, and this in spite of Captain Stanley's promise to restore William Davenport's mare to him. They took, says the Diary, 'both those that were mine owne and others that were laid to the parke . . . so not leaving me soe much as a horse either to ride on or for draught.'

    In August 1644 William Davenport was called before the Commission of Sequestration of Parliament to answer charges of delinquency. First, some of the commissioners deputed to act in the Macclesfield hundred (including two of Davenport's own tenants) arrived at Bramall Hall to take an inventory of the contents. This they did very thoroughly, searching every corner of every room and threatening to break up any box or chest not opened for them. Outside, the commissioners were guarded 'with a company of Musquettiers who stood in the parke and all about the house with their matches lighted'. Then the examination of witnesses to prove William Davenport a delinquent began. He felt sure that some of his own tenants spoke against him, and that everything which could possibly be brought against him was extorted from them. Three weeks later he was called to Stockport to answer the charges in person.

    The main accusation seems to have been that on three separate occasions William Davenport had been to meetings of the Commission of Array in Cheshire, thus showing active support for King Charles I. Davenport gave, as he thought, adequate reasons for his presence at the gatherings. He was hopeful also that his agreement with Sir William Brereton, Sir George Booth and Colonel Duckenfield, plus the fact that he had not actually used arms, would exonerate him, and that the affair would be dropped. Nevertheless he was summoned to Stockport again, about one month later, to answer further charges by the Parliamentarians. On this occasion Colonel Robert Duckenfield was present, and it was perhaps owing specially to this young man's Puritan zeal that William Davenport was pressed to take the 'National Covenant'. After a certain amount of argument, during which William Davenport declared he 'desired to have time given me in such a weighty matter, to advise with some of my friends about it', he was granted ten days' respite. At the end of this time he went to Nantwich (the Parliamentary headquarters in Cheshire) and 'satisfied the Gentlemen and Councel of Warre'.

The Parliamentarians now advised William Davenport's tenants to withhold their rents from him, and to bring their leases for examination so that a valuation of the estate could be made. (The continued persecution may be partly accounted for by the fact that Colonel Duckenfield was hard pressed for money to pay his forces that winter.) A demand for £500 'in composition' was made and, on 7 March 1645, William Davenport paid the money, not, he says, in acknowledgment of guilt, but 'thereby to buy my owne peace and rather then suffer myselfe and my estate to fall into the handes of them of whose unjust proceedings I have already had sufficient tryall, referring my future successe to the protection of the mighty god of heaven who will right me I hope in his good time'.

Even this did not conclude the matter, for, while the war in Cheshire continued, Bramall Hall continued to be used as a convenient place to quarter troops, and William Davenport was obliged to pay further instalments of £50 each, making a fine of £750 in all. He did, however, succeed in maintaining his estate intact for future generations of Davenports, and he himself lived to old age under the Commonwealth government of Oliver Cromwell.

Peter Davenport succeeded his father in 1655 and died in 1658 at the age of thirty-six. He and his wife, Anne (a member of the Legh family of Adlington), had a large family, and, true to tradition, their eldest son was named William. At least two of their children, Jenkin (born 1644) and Thomas (born 1645) were baptised in Bramall Hall chapel. Peter holds an important place in the line of Davenport descent for when, in the early-nineteenth century, the direct line came to an end, claimants to the estate arose from among the descendants of Peter's younger sons. By this time it was necessary to prove the lives and deaths of so many people in order to establish a chain of descent, that any claim had little real chance of succeeding.

Peter's eldest son – the seventh William Davenport – was only sixteen when he succeeded his father. He was hardly old enough to take an active part in Sir George Booth's abortive 'Cheshire Rising' of 1659, although he was a convinced Royalist and must have welcomed the restoration of Charles II to the throne of England the following year. In 1666 William Davenport was one of sixteen of the leading gentry who signed an agreement forming the 'Association in Cheshire', binding themselves to act together in case of any future outbreaks or rebellion against the lawful monarch.

During the later Stuart period family portrait painting was reaching a height of popularity with upper-class families, and the Davenport collection contains a number of portraits of the time. William Davenport himself was painted wearing breast- and back-plates over his tunic, and on his left shoulder a pauldron in the form of a lion's head with an almost human face. His features are those of a very young man, still almost a boy in years. There are also portraits of his wife Elizabeth (née Gregory) whom he married in 1662, and of five of their young children.

A rich tribute to the memory of the seventh William Davenport is contained in a funeral sermon preached to his memory on 26 May 1696, the day after his death. It was around Whitsuntide; the celebration of Easter not long past. In a beautiful character portrait of the man, the preacher makes this seventh William Davenport live for posterity.

> I come now to speak a few words concerning our deceased friend whom, while the memory of Christ's resurrection and ascension was fresh in our minds, and our hearts warm with the comforts arising from them, God was pleased to take to himself ... It is not my intention to play the Panegyrist upon him, wch is neither agreeable to that veneration I have for truth, nor to his modesty. I can truly say,/ and all you that knew him can bear me witness/ that he was one who to his ancient and hereditary Gentility added many eminent virtues of his own, so that he seem'd not so much to borrow lustre from his Ancestours, as to improve and embellish those ornaments they conveyed to him. He was one whose Religion did not consist in talking but in doing, a devout and assiduous worshipper of God, both publickly in the Church, and privately in his family and Closet. As true a Son of the Church of England, as any man

whatever, whose wise constitution both as to Doctrine and discipline he reverenc'd in his heart and practis'd in his Life. The office of Justice of the Peace he bare under the reign of three Kings, in whom was veryfied that old Saying, Magistratus virum indicat. For he acquir'd the just reputation of a wise and prudent magistrate, administring justice to all impartially without favour or affection. He was grievous to none, but to wicked doers, and not to their persons, so much as their vices. But a great Lover of good men, and a promoter of virtue, peace and quietness, among neighbours, as much as any man in his station; and in this blessed employment he was very successfull. His aversion to Lewd and dissolute women was singular, which made him more terrible to that sort of People than to any other. Tho' there was no sort of Evil-doer to whom he was not / as became him to be / a Terrour. His Charity to the Poor was very great, whom he fed at his door, and assisted both by his liberall hand, and by his authority; suffering no man to oppress them, or to do them wrong ... It is observable that he bare this his last Sickness with extraordinary patience and resignation to the will of God, and was seen when he thought nobody observ'd him to retire into a private corner of his Chamber, and falling upon his knees to make his supplication to God, and to commend himself, whether in Life or death, to his keeping, as unto a faithfull Creator's ... Lastly I cannot but mention, upon the assurances of those, who wou'd not deceive me, how loving a husband and tender a father he was; I will add a kind master, a sure friend, a mercifull Landlord, of a plain old English honesty, never appearing to be what he was not, but ever approving himself to be really what he professed, in word and deed ... I find some motions of Sorrow, which will not suffer me to go on farther; nor indeed is it needfull. His virtues are so well known, that his memory shall be precious to this and to the Ages to come ...

Of all the members of the Davenport family who were buried in the Davenport chapel at Stockport, to this one only is there record of a stone being laid. It was put there by William Davenport's daughter, Winefred, and bore the arms of Davenport, but, instead of the usual felon's head as crest, there was a helmet with a wreath, and, above all, a stag's head. The whole was surrounded by a border of lilies, and in each of the four corners of the stone was the outline of a human face. The inscription said, simply:

> Here lyeth the body of William Davenport of Bromhall, Esquire, who dyed May the 25. 1696.

The eighth William Davenport – eldest son of William and Elizabeth

– was thirty-three years old when he succeeded to the estate and he died ten years later. He had married Margaret, only daughter of John Warren of Poynton; for the third time in Davenport history the line at Bramhall was maintained by an alliance with the Warren family.

William Davenport's will, made in 1706 less than one month before his death, and an inventory of his goods taken just afterwards, are the only known records of him (other than his portrait) which survive. The long inventory is not totalled, but plate alone, valued at 5s. 6d. per ounce, amounted to £108 11s. 1½d. Among the rooms at Bramall Hall the inventory mentions the 'gallery', the 'gatehouse room' and the 'great gatehouse room', showing that these features of the building survived in the early-eighteenth century. There were also 'Mrs Davenport's Chamber' and 'her Closett', 'Johnathan's Room', 'Paradise', 'the nursery', 'the Chappell room' and others, besides the coach-house, the granary and outbuildings. There were 'Gardens and Orchards and ffishponds' at Bramhall and the produce from these, with the use of his goods and chattels, William Davenport left to Margaret, his wife, 'if my said wife please to live with her Children, Keeping herself unmarried and not departing from the Communion of the Church of England as by Law established In which persuasion I will and desire that my children may be educated'. He bequeathed to his wife a number of pieces of furniture and 'Also my Picture, her owne and daughter Elizabeth Davenports, and Grandfather and Grandmother Coopers'. The portraits of William Davenport and his wife (William wearing a red coat typical of the military uniform of his day) are still with the Davenport family collection, but the other portraits mentioned are not now identifiable.

In his will William Davenport expresses a desire that some of the treasures of Bramall Hall should be looked upon as heirlooms within the Davenport family. 'It is my will and minde', he said, 'that the Gilt Cupp which hath the Davenports Crest upon the Cover The Paradise Bed at Bromhall and all the furniture to that Roome All the old Pictures in the Dineing Roome Together with the large wallnut Table now at Stockport also all the Bookes belonging to my Study and the Bed therein I leave as everlasting Legacies or heire Loomes to my heires male for ever.' This injunction was largely ignored by the last Davenport of Bramhall one hundred and seventy years later – perhaps through lack of knowledge that it ever existed.

Settlement of the manor and estate must already have been made on William Davenport's eldest son, John, and no further provision was necessary in the will, but rents from various parts of the estate were set aside to provide annuities for the two younger sons and marriage portions for the four daughters. The guardianship of the young family was vested in their mother, with the trustees, chief of whom was Edward Warren, Margaret's eldest brother. 'And moreover', William Davenport's will continues, 'It is my will and minde That my younger sons if possible may be brought up Scholars, if not That then they be putt to Trades for the obtaineing a better competency of liveing . . . to prevent them from staying at home for want of Imployment.'

John, William and Warren Davenport, the three sons of the eighth William Davenport, were eleven, nine and eight years old respectively when their father died. Each one of them was to become in turn the lord of the manor of Bramhall.

Hanoverian Davenports
1706–1722	John Davenport
1722–1729	The ninth William Davenport
1729–1749	Warren Davenport
1749–1829	The tenth William Davenport

Now commences a dying-out process which was to bring the direct line of Davenport of Bramhall to an end in just over one hundred years. The seven children of William and Margaret Davenport all lived to adult years, but only three of them married. Of these three, one daughter was left a childless widow within a few months of marriage and another had one child who died at the age of nine. The only son to marry (Warren) had one child – a boy. In due course he also married, but he had no legitimate children. The collapse of the family from seven members in one generation to only one in the next was sudden, but its effects were delayed for many years because of the long life of the tenth, and last, William Davenport.

John Davenport, who succeeded his father in 1706, died unmarried when he was twenty-seven and was buried in Stockport Parish Church. His will was made on 3 May 1722, one month before his death, and it combined the disposal of his personal estate with the elaborate provisions for entail of his lands and manor more often included in a marriage settlement. As was customary, various members of the family (other than the heir) were provided for in the will by the allocation of rents of properties on the estate, and it is evident that John's widowed mother, Margaret, was still living, and his brothers and sisters still unmarried.

The legal entail of estates, which made the heir a tenant for life and ensured the succession to his eldest (perhaps yet unborn) son, was a common device among the eighteenth-century landed gentry. John Davenport would inherit such an estate and he re-entailed it for his successors. After other necessary provision had been made he left the residue of his estate 'to the use and behoofe of my loving Brother William Davenport for and during the terme of his naturall Life', but immediately after William's death 'to the use and behoofe of the ffirst Son of the said William Davenport and the heires males of the body of such ffirst Son lawfully to be begotten and for default of such Issue to the use and behoofe of the Second Son of the said William Davenport and the heires males of the body of such Second Son lawfully to be begotten and for default of such Issue to the use and behoofe of the third Son ...' and so on to the 'ffifth, Sixth, Seventh, Eighth, Ninth and all the other Sons of the said William Davenport successively one after another in Order'. Should there be no such issue of the heir, William Davenport, then John Davenport's will directed that his estate should pass 'to the use and behoofe of my loving Brother Warren Davenport for and during the terme of his natural life' with the same condition of remainder 'to the use and behoofe of the ffirst Son of the said Warren Davenport and the heires males of the body of such ffirst Son lawfully to be begotten and for default of such Issue to the use and behoofe of the Second Son ...' and so on to the 'ffourth, ffifth, Sixth, Seventh, Eighth and all other the Sons of the said Warren Davenport'. If all such issue failed then the estate would pass to the girls of the family, named in order of seniority, 'and their heires for ever'.

Powers were given to John's brothers William and Warren, if in possession of the estate, to make provision for their younger children by allocation to them of income as approved by the trustees, and also to make jointure settlement for 'such Women as shall be their respective Wives'. The cash value of a wife is assessed in advance. For every £100 which the wife brings with her as dowry she is entitled to a £10 'jointure'.

A few sentences at the end of this elaborately-worded settlement disposed of John Davenport's personal bequests. 'I give and devise to my Brother William Davenport my two old Silver cups mention'd in my ffather's Will together with all the heir Loomes now in my house att Bramhall'. To Warren he left 'my best silver Tankard and one silver pint cup and ffour small silver punch cups or Tumblers and any of my horses Mares or Geldings which he shall chuse after my decease'.

No known source sheds further light on the pattern of John's life. We have only this glimpse of a young man, unmarried, 'being weak in body butt of sound and perfect Mind and Memory' speedily making the arrangements necessary to ensure that his lands shall pass without question to his brother and his brother's heirs.

The ninth William Davenport was twenty-five years old when he inherited the manor of Bramhall. He died unmarried at the age of thirty-two. No further provision for settlement of the estate was necessary, for the succession was assured to his younger brother, Warren.

In accordance with his father's desire, Warren Davenport was brought up 'a scholar', being sent to Brasenose College, Oxford, when he was sixteen. He obtained a B.A. degree three years later, and entered the Church, but how he fared in this calling goes unrecorded. For twenty years he was lord of the manor of Bramhall, dying in 1749 at the age of nearly fifty-one.

Several known dates record work done in Bramall Hall and on the estate during Rev. Warren Davenport's time. The chained prayer books, dated 1737, would be introduced into the chapel by him, though generally speaking the practice of having chained books in churches was now becoming out of date and largely discontinued. His initials and the date 1739 were to be found on the dial of a clock built on to the outside of the south wall, near the chapel,[14] where it would be clearly visible to intending worshippers. And, like many other clergymen both of his time and later, Warren Davenport was among the first to show a sense of responsibility for the education of the children of the poor in his locality. He established a school on Bramhall Green, just opposite to Bramall Hall gates, and on the building was the inscription 'This school was built at the expense of Warren Davenport, clerk and Esquire, in the year 1741'.[15] Finally, it is recorded that on one of the tie-beams of the upper storey of the north wing, originally open to the roof from end to end and forming a dormitory for the servants, was daubed in white paint 'This Plaise was repar'd Aug 1746'.[16] This repair took place during Warren Davenport's short married life and should, perhaps, be credited to his wife.

When he was in his forty-sixth year Rev. Warren Davenport married Achsah, daughter of Caleb Storrs of Stockport, a Quaker and a member of the Cheshire Meeting of the Society of Friends. The wedding was by special licence at Marple, and was conducted by Rev. Robert Berks, an elderly clergyman who had been many years curate in charge. As a preliminary to the ceremony he baptised Achsah, whom he described in the register as 'a woman of ripe years'.[17] Achsah was then thirty-two years old. She had five and a half years of married life and forty-eight of widowhood.

A son was born to Warren and Achsah on 18 November 1745. He was called 'William' in the family tradition. He was less than four years old when his father died.

The tenth William Davenport held the Bramhall estates for a longer period of time than any of his predecessors; from his fourth to his eighty-fourth year he was lord of the manor of Bramhall. His legal guardians during his long minority were Peter Legh of Lyme, Charles Legh of Adlington, Joseph Marshall of Doncaster (a Quaker) and his mother, Achsah Davenport.

In April 1767, a few months after he had become of age, William married Martha, the youngest daughter of Rev. John Le Tourcey, Rector of Hesset in Suffolk. The year before their marriage the portraits of both William and Martha were painted by 'Mr Tate'.[18] William Tate, a well-known portrait-painter of the time, practised in Manchester as well as London. His Davenport portraits have a background of rural scenery and blue sky which was fashionable at the time. William Davenport is shown with his arm resting on a piece of music, probably indicating that he was fond of music. Martha Le Tourcey has a hint of coquetry, and is undoubtedly a beauty.

William and Martha had no children.

Substantial alterations to Bramall Hall took place during this last William Davenport's lordship. The gatehouse side (built originally for defence) was now neither necessary nor fashionable. According to a description of about 1774 'This house was originally built round a court, but the present owner (William Davenport, Esq.) has wisely taken down one useless side and made it both more pleasant and more healthful'.[19] William Davenport also took down the long gallery, perhaps because it was not now considered safe, though this did not take place until many years after the removal of the gatehouse side. The gallery is shown, from the east and from the west, in two engravings by Peter de Wint which were copied from George Ormerod's original sketches of 1809, made for his history of Cheshire. Ormerod says that the fourth side of the building 'was removed by the present proprietor, who has also taken down a long gallery which extended along the top of the eastern side, and added much to the imposing effect of the building.'[20] His wording could suggest that when he wrote (1819) the long gallery had only recently been taken down.

The gallery was certainly in existence in 1790, for it was seen by John Byng (later fifth Viscount Torrington), whose holiday travels took him through Bramhall and whose impressions were recorded in his intimate journal.[21] Byng's tour of the Midlands that summer took him as far north as Buxton, where he stayed several days. On Monday, 21 June 1790, Byng set off for Manchester, taking in Bramall Hall on his way, for it was not uncommon for gentlemen on tour to arrive unannounced at the historic homes of the gentry, in the hope of being able to view and perhaps (privately) to criticise them.

As Byng approached Bramall Hall he saw 'the owner, Mr Davenport, whose family have been long seated here; and are of great antiquity in this county'. 'My reception', he added, 'was very civil into this oldest of all the striped houses'. Byng's use of the word 'striped' may be the earliest known reference to the special 'black and white' treatment given to the half-timbered houses of Cheshire.[22] 'Black and white', he wrote, 'flourish'd into as many devices as a boy wou'd draw upon his kite.' He was shown round the house by a servant-maid, a not unusual guide for an unexpected visitor to a country mansion. Byng's account of the interior is written in a light-heartedly critical vein, and gives a penetrating glimpse into the domestic attitudes of William and Martha Davenport. 'The situation is good, so are the views', he wrote, 'but taste has been little consulted; and the servant maid, whom I beg'd to show me every antiquity, said that her master loved antiquity, but her mistress the modern taste.'

He noted that 'the fine old drawing room, up stairs, and the other inhabited rooms have been lately modernly sash'd! (Cou'd no one have convinced Mr D., (or Mrs D.,) that an old house might be newly sash'd, without quitting the antique taste, and be made as elegant, and commodious, as possible.)' There are no sashed windows in Bramall Hall now, but two drawings dated 1826, which belong to Capesthorne Hall, bear out Byng's statement. These drawings by J. C. Buckler, the artist-architect, clearly show sashed windows in the withdrawing room and in some other rooms, though not in the great hall or the paradise room. The withdrawing room windows – the work of (to quote Byng) 'Mr D. (or Mrs D.)' – were subsequently restored to their original state, probably by a later Davenport.

'The servant then took me at my desire, to the long gallery up stairs . . .' Here Byng saw 'old armour, saddles, and curiously-wrought massive stirrups, that shou'd be repair'd, and hung up in the hall; (or given to me)'. There was also a chest of old books which Byng coveted for himself. 'If gentlemen have no taste themselves, why not consult, or bestow upon, others?' he wrote, in the airy, self-confident tone which characterises his criticisms.

'The rooms for use', he said, 'are trick'd up a la mode; and from one, Mrs D. came forth, with very civil deportment.' She seems to have made a somewhat unfavourable impression upon Byng! He was shown into the old chapel, which, he found, was 'undergoing (a good phrase) a repair; let me see it then, e'er the repair be accomplish'd'. He noted that 'it is very low, and ancient; they are smearing the wood work with a composition. The books are all fasten'd by chains'. He also saw in the chapel 'much stain'd glass; as there also was in many of the house windows, much of which is removed into Mr D.'s dressing room.'

His conclusion is that 'Mr D. has had bad advice; or lacks taste; or is under management!!!' It is easy to guess which of these alternatives Byng favours, though so short a visit (he was off to Cheadle, Altrincham and Dunham Massey, before putting up for the night at the Bridgewater Arms, Manchester) could hardly give him firm grounds for an opinion.

William and Martha had been married for twenty-three years when John Byng recorded his sight-seeing visit to Bramall Hall, and it must have been long apparent that they would have no son to inherit the estate. William Davenport had, however, two natural daughters, whom he adopted and brought up at Bramall Hall. According to the findings of Alfred Burton in his search for information one hundred years later, their mother was Peggy Brooke who lived at the old timber-framed cottage at the entrance to 'Benja Fold'. This information Burton obtained from three local residents.[23] He also quotes, without comment, a note which he had seen on a manuscript in Chetham's Library, Manchester. It is written in a small hand on the title-page of a mid-nineteenth-century manuscript which appears otherwise to have nothing to do with the Davenports, and reads 'Margaret Brown of Stockport (commonly known by the name of "dirty Peg" was the female by whom Wm. Davenport of Bramhall, Esq., had two illegitimate daughters . . .'[24] Immediately above the name 'Brown' has been written in pencil, and apparently in a different hand, '?Brooke'. It is difficult to know what reliance, if any, to place upon this note, for it does not seem to refer to the same person, and the information from local residents should be more authentic. The note does show the type of speculation rife during the lifetime of both William Davenport and his adopted daughters.

The surname of the daughters was certainly 'Brooke' and not 'Brown'; Earwaker in his genealogical table of the Davenport of Bramhall family, gives the name as 'Brooke, alias Davenport'. Maria was born on 10 April 1785; Anne, her sister, was a year or two older. In 1806 Anne married Samuel Hunt, her father's coachman − a mesalliance according to the views of that time, and against her father's consent. Maria, the younger daughter, was married on 31 May 1810, when she was twenty-five years of age, to a naval officer, Captain Salusbury Pryce Humphreys. She became her father's heiress, and her husband made his home in Bramall Hall.

William Davenport's wife, Martha, died on Christmas Day, 1810, seven months after Maria's wedding at Stockport Parish Church. Martha Davenport was buried in a vault specially constructed at the east end of Bramall Hall chapel. Hers is the first known interment in the chapel at Bramhall. Perhaps the rebuilding of Stockport Parish Church which was then imminent − and which ultimately involved the abolition of the four family chapels − provided a reason for this change of burial place for the Davenports.

William Davenport himself lived to see a new blossoming of his family. Five sons and two daughters were born to his daughter, Maria, and her husband, and the name chosen for the first-born was according to family tradition, the boy becoming 'William Davenport Humphreys'. He was seventeen years old when his grandfather died.

The tenth William Davenport died on 14 April 1829 and was buried in the vault in the chapel at Bramall Hall. The ceremony was 'strictly private, and confined entirely to the party invited and the servants of the Household', the principal mourners being 'Captain Humphreys' and 'Master Humphreys'.[25]

Chapter 4   DAVENPORT OF BRAMHALL – the break in the line

Salusbury Pryce Humphreys was born in 1778, the third son of the Rector of Montgomery in North Wales and Clungunford, near Ludlow.[1] At the early age of twelve he entered the Navy and very soon gained promotion, but though he became noted for his daring and bravery his active naval career came very quickly to an end in 1807. The occasion of his downfall was the *Chesapeake* and *Leopard* incident of June that year, which was one of the contributory causes of war in 1812 between England and the newly-formed United States of America.

In 1806 Captain Humphreys was appointed to the command of H.M.S. *Leopard* and the following year the ship was sent to serve in American seas. The Napoleonic war was at its height and relations between Britain and America had become somewhat strained, the position being aggravated by the British policy of impressment for the Navy. Many a sailor forced against his will into the British Navy would find a means of escape by deserting to America and perhaps changing his name. Some might even manage to change their nationality according to American laws, but to Britain they were all deserters, to be searched out and punished with the utmost rigour.

On 1 June 1807 Vice-Admiral Berkeley, who was in charge of the British fleet in American seas, issued instructions to the ships under his command to search the American frigate *Chesapeake* for British deserters, should she appear outside the limits of American waters. When, therefore, Captain Humphreys of the *Leopard* sighted the *Chesapeake* off the Capes of Virginia, he demanded the right of search; when search was refused he opened fire, and a short engagement took place in which some members of the *Chesapeake* were killed and others injured. The American ship then hauled down her colours; the officers of the *Leopard* boarded her, and they took off four men – the claimed deserters.

This incident caused a turmoil of public feeling in both countries out of all proportion to its real importance. The chief parties involved were immediately removed from their commands, the commodore of the American vessel being suspended without pay for five years because of the insult he had allowed to be inflicted on him, and Vice-Admiral Berkeley and Captain Humphreys both being recalled by the British Government in an effort to conciliate the United States. Berkeley was reinstated in a similar command, and later retired with honour and with the rank of admiral. Not so Salusbury Pryce Humphreys. His applications for renewed service were continually disregarded and he never saw active service again.

At the time of his recall from service Salusbury Pryce Humphreys was already married and had a son a few months old. His first wife died the following year and her estates were settled on her child. Captain Humphreys' marriage in 1810 was to another heiress, Maria Davenport. He settled at Bramall Hall, and long before the death of his father-in-law, the tenth William Davenport, Captain Humphreys had become an influential and respected figure in Stockport and district. He was a justice of the peace for the county of Cheshire and, later, for the borough of Stockport, a founder member of the Stockport Savings Bank and of the Stockport branch of the District Bank, and involved in many other aspects of public life.

After the accession in 1830 of William IV, the 'sailor king' with whom Humphreys had served for a time as a midshipman in the Navy, some national recognition and long-delayed honours began to come his way. On 26 September 1831 he was made a Knight Companion of the Bath, and on 21 February 1834 a Knight Commander of the Royal Guelphic Order (a Hanoverian order conferred only by George IV and his brother William IV). On 10 January 1837 Humphreys was promoted to flag rank in the Navy and became a Rear-Admiral of the Blue and, finally, by brevet issued after the birth of Queen Victoria's first child in November 1841, he was made Rear-Admiral of the White. The honours were in form only, for the Rear-Admiral was now on retired half-pay.

In 1829 Captain Humphreys (as he then was) came into possession of the Bramhall estate by right of his wife, for a married woman could not hold property in her own name. During the years that followed it seemed as though his ownership might be challenged by members of the legitimate branch of the Davenport family who claimed that blood relationship with the late William Davenport gave them a prior right to the estate. One member of the family went so far as to take his case to the courts. He was

Edmund Davenport, a man in humble circumstances, and he brought an ejectment case against Sir Salusbury Pryce Humphreys in 1835.[2]

There were now no living, legitimate descendants of the last two generations of the Davenport family of Bramhall, and no male descendants of the third generation back. The ancestry claimed by Edmund Davenport came through Thomas, the third son of Peter Davenport of Commonwealth days. Edmund made two attempts to prove his case. He failed in the Court of Chancery where he claimed to be heir 'in tail male' to Peter, for no entail was found to have been made. He tried again at the Nisi Prius court at the Chester Assizes of August 1835. Here he claimed only to be heir 'in fee simple' to the tenth William Davenport who died in 1829 and who (so the case went) had left to his adopted daughter only those lands which he himself had purchased, retaining the estate for the Davenport family 'as was the constant practice with the old Cheshire families, who were proud, and justly proud, of transmitting the family estates in long lines of ancestry, from generation to generation.' An attempt was made to prove a pedigree, not only upwards from William Davenport to Peter, the common ancestor, but also down again from Peter through Thomas, to Edmund, the so-called 'heir-at-law' of Bramhall. The only witness to be called on Edmund's behalf was an elderly uncle, James Davenport, and his evidence was very vague. On the other hand the evidence for Sir Salusbury Pryce Humphreys was clear and unassailable. His solicitor produced deeds of conveyance dated 9 and 10 October 1820 whereby William Davenport left all his manor and lands, in Bramhall and elsewhere, in trust for (in the first place) Salusbury Pryce Humphreys, then for Maria (in the event of the earlier death of her husband), and then for the children of Salusbury and Maria.

The result of the case was a disaster for Edmund Davenport. He was already in prison for non-payment of costs of his previous case, and it is said he died there a few years later.

In May 1838, when he was nearly sixty years of age, Sir Salusbury Pryce Humphreys assumed the name of 'Davenport' by Royal Licence. It was nine years since the death of William Davenport who, in leaving the estate to his son-in-law and natural daughter, had made no conditions whatsoever; the change of name was not, therefore, obligatory. Sir Salusbury Davenport, as he now became, and his wife, Maria, must have hoped by this Royal Licence to ensure the continuation of the family name at Bramhall; in fact the line of Davenport lasted for another forty years only.

It is not difficult to deduce that one of the reasons for the failure of the Davenport tenure must have been financial. An examination of the Abstract of Title of the last Davenport of Bramhall to Bramall Hall provides the evidence, and it is on Admiral Sir Salusbury Davenport that the main burden of responsibility must lie. He expended large sums of money in his private living and, after his death, the *Stockport Advertiser* referred to 'his munificent gifts to all our public institutions' as well as to 'his private charities, which were numerous and unostentatious'.[3] But the mortgages owing at his death became the problem of his successors.

A peep into the magnificent living of Salusbury and Maria is given in an unpublished diary of the time, written later in the year in which Sir Salusbury assumed the name of 'Davenport'.[4] Charles Bellairs, the author of the diary, was the younger son of a country clergyman and up at Oxford on a very small allowance. There he met Thomas Bradshawe Isherwood, the only son of a country gentleman and obviously (from Bellairs's somewhat worldly-wise point of view) a very desirable friend. During the summer term of 1838 Charles Bellairs also met the mother of his friend and two of his sisters ('one of whom' wrote Bellairs, 'I afterwards married'), and he was delighted to receive an invitation to their home at Marple Hall before the end of the long vacation.

Marple Hall was about five miles from Bramall Hall, and was situated on an almost precipitious edge of the Goyt valley. Its owner in 1838 was John Bradshawe Isherwood, a descendant of that family whose outstanding member had been John Bradshawe, President of the High Court of Justice which condemned King Charles I to death. To the Squire of Marple ('an old Gentleman ... rather stout and rosy') fell the duty of entertaining their guest, for his son Thomas was ill, and part of the entertainment proved to be an invitation to dinner with the Davenports at Bramall Hall.

A daughter of Salusbury and Maria Davenport (probably Emily, born in 1813) was friendly with Squire Isherwood's own three daughters, and she was with them at Marple on the day of Bellairs's arrival. Before introducing his guest to the four young ladies, who were 'in their own little Parlour, which was rather shabbily furnished', the Squire named and described his daughters, and then he added:

> 'Besides these three you will find with them their great friend and companion Miss Davenport, the daughter of my neighbour Sir Salusbury Davenport who has invited you to dinner tomorrow when you will see his fine old place. The Rental of his estate, Sir, is about the same as mine but

> still I would not change with him. I should not like his daughter to hear it, but I believe his estate is mortgaged which naturally diminishes his income, and as he lives at much greater expense than I do, I am afraid he is at times inconvenienced.'

Later, when they were alone together again, Squire Isherwood remarked to Bellairs: 'Miss Davenport's Mother, Sir, was a considerable heiress, and I have reason to believe that I might have married her myself in which case my property would have been doubled what it is now'. He then mentioned for the first time that his own wife was not at home. 'She is gone to the seaside, Sir, with her maid. She frequently goes for two or three months together, but I have so many home occupations, I do not much miss her.'

The next morning, after breakfast, the Squire offered to show his guest over the principal rooms of Marple Hall. Gazing through the large bay window of the drawing room, they saw the tall chimney of a factory about a mile distant.

> 'That', he [the Squire] said, 'is the great drawback to the landscape before you. The piece of landscape on which the factory is built formed part of this estate, but my eldest brother who then owned it, and who was too fond of horses and dogs, and who had entire control over the estate was obliged to sell nearly a thousand acres to discharge his debts, and amongst them that piece which is now in view of these windows'.

He then added:

> 'If I had married Lady Davenport as I believe I might have done, there would have been more than twice a thousand acres added to the estate, and I don't suppose I should have been required to have her name as Sir Salusbury has done, for as my family is as old as hers, and as I already have two sur-names, I do not think I should have been expected to take a third. You will see Lady Davenport this evening, Sir, a charming person but I grieve to think they must be living beyond their income, and I greatly fear (as I said before) that we shall before long see the result of it, and now, Sir, I will just shew you the two guest chambers which are usually shewn to visitors, and also my wife's private sitting-room and then I must start for Manchester, and I shall return home at night by way of my friend Sir Salusbury's, who has kindly undertaken to send a carriage to convey you, and the girls there, during the afternoon.'

After their tour of the house, Bellairs saw his host into the large, yellowish-brown carriage which 'the Girls' had nicknamed 'Bumble Bee', and off went the old Squire to his Agricultural Dinner in Manchester.

Bellairs thus recorded the evening's outing to Bramhall:

> In the evening we drove off in Sir Salusbury's carriage for the dinner party at his grand old place of which I shall say no more as it is fully described in every Cheshire Guide Book, and there are several views of it in Nash's Mansions. It is one of the finest specimens in England of a Tudor House, and has the handsomest Drawing-room in Cheshire.
>
> There was a party of about twenty-four to dinner: all the military from the neighbouring town, the Rector and his wife, the Curate and his wife, the Lawyer and his wife, and the remainder made up of the neighbouring Gentry.
>
> We dined in the Great Entrance Hall and after dinner it was proposed, as there were several officers, one of whom I was told (a Sir Michael Somebody) had at that moment two bullets inside him, that there should be an impromptu dance in a room adjoining the Hall, and whilst we were in the middle of it, the old Squire and Bumble were announced on the way from the Manchester Agricultural dinner and we were told that the horses must not be kept in the cold.
>
> I overheard the old Gentleman tell Lady Davenport that he was pleased with his son's College friend, and that I was respectful, and not over-talkative, and that when I had passed my 'little go' he intended to invite me again, for he said it was agreeable to find a young man in the present day who knew how to behave to his elders.

It seems a pity that Charles Bellairs, who was so astute a portrayer of character in the case of his Marple host, left no first-hand impression of the characters of Salusbury and Maria Davenport. All his thoughts were obviously at Marple, and the occasional sideways glance at himself betokens his concern for the effect he was creating on the family there. His full reports of the conversation of his host do, however, cast an interesting reflection on the character of Maria. John Bradshawe Isherwood showed a regard for Lady Davenport not entirely accounted for by the fact that she had once been 'a considerable heiress'. He called her 'a charming person', and treated her as one whose judgment he trusted and in whom he could confide his views of his visitor's eligibility, for it is obvious that on both sides this visit of Bellairs to Marple was being treated as a test of suitability for marriage.

In 1841 Salusbury and Maria Davenport left Bramall Hall for Bath Buildings, Cheltenham, where they lived for the next four-and-a-half years. Perhaps the move confirms the Squire of Marple's prediction as to the result of over-expensive living; perhaps it was for health reasons. Here Sir Salusbury died on 17 November 1845 and he was buried nearby, in

Leckhampton churchyard, by his own written desire.

During the last years of Sir Salusbury Davenport's life, or in the years immediately following his death, the sale of the Bramhall estate must have been seriously considered by the Davenport family.[5] Legal ownership passed to the widow, Maria Davenport, but the negotiations for sale were undertaken by her eldest son. The possible purchaser seems to have been John Davenport of Leek, one of the Staffordshire Davenports famous for their pottery, but the negotiations fell through and he later bought the Foxley estate in Herefordshire. About the year 1850 Lady Davenport offered building land for sale on the north and west boundaries of the Bramhall estate. A plan shows the land divided into building plots; the western area adjoining Bramall Park was 'judiciously laid out in plots for Villas' and the northern part, on either side of Bramhall Lane in the Charlestown and Woodsmoor areas, 'laid out extensively for the erection of respectable buildings'.[6] The Davenport family do not seem to have been much in residence at Bramall Hall in the 1840s and the building was probably let. It is described in Slater's directory of 1848 as 'now in the occupation of Robert Sharp, Esq.', who had also been there at the time of the 1841 census.

In 1847 William Davenport Davenport (born William Davenport Humphreys), the eldest son of Salusbury and Maria, retired from the Army with the rank of Major. He was a widower with one young daughter, his first wife, whom he had married in Malta, having died there in 1845. On 24 October 1850 he married for the second time. His bride was Diana Elizabeth Handley, daughter of John Handley of Muskham Grange, Newark, a member of a wealthy Nottinghamshire banking family. The couple settled at Bramall Hall and in 1854 Maria Davenport legally transferred the Bramhall estate to her eldest son, retaining only a small annuity for herself. During the remaining years of her life she lived in London with her youngest son, Charles Edgcumbe Davenport, and there she died in 1866, when she was in her eighty-second year. She was buried in Kensal Green cemetery.

William Davenport Davenport's earlier army service with the Cameronians had taken him to many parts of the world; he had further and unexpected opportunity for service at home during the years 1853–1855.

He was commissioned to raise a second regiment of county militia in Cheshire (necessary in order to maintain the home-based forces and relieve the regular army for service in the Crimean War), and he became its Lieutenant-Colonel Commandant.

The first headquarters of the regiment was at Stockport, but the assembling of men for their annual period of training was deferred in October 1853 because of the outbreak of cholera which threatened the town. Next year the regiment assembled in Chester for training, and it was made known – much to the displeasure of the Stockport Borough Council – that the headquarters was to be moved to Chester. Soon after training, the regiment was sent to Plymouth and then to Devonport where, in November 1855, the presentation of the colours took place. This duty fell to Mrs Davenport, but, from the report in the *Stockport Advertiser*, it is her husband who emerges as the colourful character. 'The gallant Colonel mounted his charger, and in a clear and sonorous tone, that made his words audible to the surrounding soldiers, delivered a brief but spirited speech on the occasion.' He thus addressed his regiment: 'Those colours now presented to you, which you will ever raise with stout hearts and brawny arms, you will I know, defend to the last . . . Should the service of the 2nd Royal Cheshire be required, the answer is on our lips: "Ready!" aye "Ready!" always "Ready to serve our Queen and country in any part of the country in any part of the world." . . . And as long as I have health and strength, by Heavens! I will remain with you to the last!'[7]

In civil life William Davenport Davenport served as a justice of the peace and as Deputy Lieutenant of the county of Cheshire. The interested visitor to Bramall Hall was welcomed, as in the days of the Colonel's grandfather, the tenth William Davenport. 'I believe that the present proprietor, with a liberality worthy of a genuine country squire, throws no obstacles in the way of parties who may wish to see the place, and come with a determination to demean themselves becomingly', said a writer of 1855, recommending Bramall Hall as a place offering many attractions to the rambler, who could now reach it in about ten minutes from the station of Bramhall on the Macclesfield branch of the London & North Western Railway.[8]

Religious services were still held regularly in the chapel at Bramall Hall; indeed, these services formed part of the amenities of the district for they were specially mentioned in Maria Davenport's offer of building land for sale. 'The English Church Service is regularly performed every Sunday Afternoon, in the Domestic Chapel at Bramall Hall, which would be open for families residing in the vicinity', ran the advertisement accompanying the building plan.[9] Bramhall at this time was in process of being transferred from the ecclesiastical parish of St Mary, Stockport, to that of St Thomas, and a clergyman from St Thomas's came out to conduct service at Bramhall. In reminiscences to Reginald Dean many years later a lady of ninety recalled how, during her early childhood in the 1860s, she was taken to worship in Bramall Hall chapel every Sunday afternoon. She remembered in particular an occasion when a young boy fell asleep during the service, and Mr Davenport said that he should not be disturbed.[10]

Colonel Davenport died on 21 February 1869 and was buried in the vault at the east end of Bramall Hall chapel. The funeral service was strictly private, being attended only by members of the family, a portion of the tenantry and the servants. 'The Rev. J. Taylor read the Burial Service with much emotion', wrote the *Stockport Advertiser*, 'and the body was consigned to its last resting-place close to the spot where so often its immortal spirit had come to worship whilst in the flesh. The tears and sobs of many present told how great was the loss they had sustained, and by none was the feeling so strongly displayed as by the domestics who had been in long and close intercourse with the departed, and knew well his kindness of heart and sterling worth.'[11] Before the funeral took place the coffin, covered only with two wreaths of evergreens, lay in state in the billiard room (the downstairs banqueting hall). When the service was over those residents of Bramhall who had congregated in the courtyard to witness the funeral procession, filed into the chapel to pay their last respects to their squire before the vault was closed.

The heir, John William Handley Davenport, was a young man of seventeen, the only child of Colonel Davenport by his second wife, Diana Elizabeth. By the terms of his father's will[12] the estate was put under the management of trustees until he attained his twenty-fifth birthday. They were authorised to let Bramall Hall and to apply the proceeds towards the upkeep of the property and the discharge of mortgages. The three trustees originally appointed by the will of 1857 were the boy's mother, Diana Elizabeth Davenport, and his two uncles, John and Philip Handley of Newark-on-Trent. Less than three months before his death William Davenport Davenport, now a sick man, made a codicil to his will removing his wife from her position as an executor and trustee. In her place Colonel Davenport named his son-in-law, Frederick Augustus Williamson, the husband of Maria Dorothea, his daughter by his first wife.

One can only infer that there had been some estrangement between Colonel Davenport and his wife, or that infirmity of some kind prevented her from acting as a trustee of the estate. She had not predeceased her husband; according to the Davenport pedigree roll she outlived him by thirty years. The only clue to her elusive character is a portrait – the last in date of the Davenport of Bramhall collection – showing a handsome woman in widow's dress of the Victorian period and dated December 1870, nearly two years after the death of her husband.

During the seven years following Colonel Davenport's death Frederick Williamson acted alone as executor of the will, trustee of the estate, and guardian of his step-brother-in-law. The brothers John and Philip Handley refused to serve. By special indenture made between themselves and Frederick Williamson they renounced the office of executors and all other benefits or powers which might have come to them under the will.[13]

Concerning the young heir himself during the years 1869 to 1877, information is scant. He had been educated at Rugby School and he was entered at Magdalene College, Cambridge, in the autumn of 1869, though he did not obtain a degree. He is shown as a 'visitor' at Bramall Hall on the census return of 1871 but, for obvious reasons, this could not be his permanent residence; nor could Mile End Hall, in Stockport, which once had been a subsidiary residence of the Davenport family but no longer formed part of the estate. Wallbank Hill, a house standing on a high bank overlooking the valley of the Ladybrook eastwards from Bramall Hall, had once been a jointure house of the Davenports, but there is no evidence that John William Handley Davenport lived there. That he was concerned with the extensions to the barn and shippon at Wallbank is evidenced by a stone, bearing his initials and the date 1874, which was built in on the north side. The barn and shippon are no longer standing, but the stone with its inscription JWHD can still be seen, now incorporated into the fabric of the

AD
1874

house on its eastern side.[14] In the same year, 1874, the Bramhall School Board was formed, with John William Handley Davenport as its first chairman, and about this time he took his seat on the bench as a justice of the peace for Cheshire. By 1876 he was listed in Slater's directory among the gentry of Stockport, and here his address is given as 'Ack Lane, Bramhall'.

Whatever may have been the feelings of Colonel Davenport concerning the possible sale of Bramall Hall in the 1840s, he was obviously determined, when he made his will in 1857, that the family name and ownership should continue there after his death. Should his son fail to inherit, he made provision for the property to pass to any other children he might have, including his daughter, or, failing them, through his younger brothers. In a long and closely-written document he made arrangements (so it would seem) for every contingency of succession. He even directed that anyone coming into possession of the estate under the provision of his will who did not already bear the name of 'Davenport' should endeavour by Royal Licence to take that name, 'so that the name of "Davenport" shall be the last and principal name', and that anyone so inheriting who already bore the name of 'Davenport' must keep that name.

The contingency which Colonel Davenport and his legal advisers did not foresee was that which actually occurred. His son, within five months of obtaining undisputed ownership of the property, sold the manor of Bramhall and, a few years later, took his mother's maiden name in addition to his own, putting the surname of 'Handley' and not that of 'Davenport' as the 'last and principal name'.

Chapter 5   INTERLUDE

During the years 1869 to 1876 Bramall Hall became the home of Wakefield Christy, a member of the famous hatting firm, who for business reasons had to live near Stockport. It was when he was only twenty-four years old, and still a bachelor, that Wakefield Christy, the great-grandson of Miller Christy, founder of the firm of Christy & Co. in London, was sent to Stockport in order to supervise production at the Stockport factory of his company. His first home was at Hillgate House, the Stockport property of his firm, and he was joined there by his mother, his younger brother, Stephen, and his unmarried sister, Ellen Sophia.

Almost immediately after Colonel Davenport's death the Christy family took the seven-year lease of Bramall Hall, paying a rental of £125 per quarter. The account books kept by Wakefield Christy during his tenancy show that his farm stock included cows, pigs and poultry and (in the later years) sheep. Some grassland was let for ley and milk production and the sale of milk formed an important part of his farming activities.

In 1872 Wakefield Christy, now thirty-six years of age, married Mary Elizabeth Richardson, daughter of Jonathan Joseph Richardson of Kircassock, County Down, and, on her mother's side, a member of that branch of the Christy family which had many years earlier settled in Northern Ireland. The wedding took place on Wednesday, 28 August 1872, at Kircassock, and the bride and bridegroom left to spend their honeymoon on the Continent, but other members of the Christy and Richardson families returned to Bramhall where they had further responsibility for entertainment to come. Wakefield Christy had planned extensive celebrations at Bramall Hall for his friends and for the Stockport employees of his firm.

The Stockport works of Christy & Co. closed down that Friday evening so that all hands could take part in the festivities on the following day, Saturday 31 August 1872. Every employee had received an invitation card printed in blue and gold, at the top of which was an engraving of Bramall Hall. Beneath the personal invitation from Mr Wakefield Christy were the words:

This invitation is extended to those he has long known and worked with,
and whose co-operation and good will he so much values.

With the invitation went a small strip of tear-off tickets. These entitled the
holder in turn to 'Wine', 'Dinner alley', 'Wine', 'Refreshment', 'Tea alley'
and 'Refreshment'.

A very full account of the proceedings on this festive day appeared in
both the *Stockport Advertiser* and the *Stockport & Cheshire County News*.
In the morning the employees of Christy & Co. and the elder scholars of St
Thomas's Sunday School, accompanied by two bands, marched in
procession from the Stockport works to Bramall Hall. The great length of
the procession attracted the interest of many spectators. There was rain at
first in Stockport, and umbrellas and coats were in evidence, but the sun
came out in strength as the procession entered the Park from the Bramhall
Lane end. Streamers and flags and other decorations had been fitted up at
the gates to welcome the guests. Dinner was due to be served at noon, and
before this time guests were free to stroll through the woods, watch the
performances of 'Punch and Judy' or partake of liquid refreshment in the
great tent which had been erected just near the Hall. A motto inside this
tent warned the over-enthusiastic: 'May today's diversions bear
tomorrow's reflections'!

Mid-day dinner was the great event of the day, and the arrangements
had been so meticulously made, and were so satisfactorily carried out, that
two thousand one hundred and twenty people were able to dine at one
sitting. The principal tent was 170 ft long and 70 ft wide, and
accommodated one hundred and eighty persons. The second dining tent,
which was divided from the first by a wide passage, was 102 ft by 45 ft,
and there were several smaller tents. The decorations included lovers' knots
in cloth, flags, and a great motto 'God bless the Bride and Bridegroom'.
Members of the two families, with the chief guests, sat at a table at the
south end of the principal tent;[1] other guests occupied long tables running
the whole length of the tent. Concerning the dinner itself the reporter for the
County News remarked, 'If we may judge by the great clatter of knives,
forks and plates, we should say that the bracing country air had
considerably sharpened the appetites of the guests, and certainly the three
oxen which had fallen a sacrifice to the nuptial celebrations received "no
quarter". There was also an ample supply of mutton and lamb, and beer
was served from tea urns *ad libitum*. The 200 plum puddings were
despatched with equal gusto, and the brandy sauce found a ready market.

After dinner the bugle sounded for silence, and Stephen Christy, Esq. [the bridegroom's brother], who presided, rose amid great cheering to propose the toast of "Her Most Gracious Majesty the Queen" '. [2]

The loyal toast was drunk and the National Anthem was sung. After this Mr William Tipping, member of Parliament for Stockport and a personal friend of the bridegroom, proposed the health of the happy couple in a long speech, regularly punctuated with applause from the audience and cries of 'Hear, hear'. He praised the bridegroom's application to his business, and to the duties of life, 'instead of giving way to the frivolities of youth', and his devotion to the great concern of which he was now the head. 'And let me tell you', continued Mr Tipping, 'more than once in our frequent chats I have told him it was time to marry. In the strength of his will, in his devotion to business, he has said "Oh, I am not of a marrying sort!".' Although neither he – Mr Tipping – nor the majority of those present had yet met the lady whom Mr Christy had chosen to be his bride, he knew that 'Mr Wakefield Christy is not the man to make a mistake even in matrimony; and I'll answer for it, that once more he has succeeded again.' Finally, Mr Tipping dared to conclude his good wishes for the couple's happiness with the hope that 'twelve months hence, some one may see Mrs Christy, the loving mother, looking fondly into a cradle', which induced the guests, after the toasts had been drunk and three hearty cheers given for the bride and bridegroom, to add a fourth cheer for 'the little one'.

During part of the afternoon the interior of Bramall Hall was open for the inspection of guests, and the wedding presents were displayed on the billiard table. 'Being very rich and valuable, they were greatly admired', said the *County News*. At the head of the table was placed the solid silver punch bowl (specially made and inscribed by Elkington of Manchester) which had been presented to Wakefield Christy and his bride by the Stockport employees of Christy & Co.

The main activities during the rest of the afternoon centred on the sports and athletics contests which had been arranged for the work people. The three-legged race turned out to be not nearly so amusing as expected, because no-one was unfortunate enough to fall, but the steeplechase, which involved crossing the brook, created a great deal of excitement. Of the three starters, not one cleared the brook. They 'dropped into the water and scrambled out as best they could', and it obviously caused the spectators much amusement to behold 'the difficulty of running a race in clothing thoroughly saturated with water'! [3] When the events had all been run the prizes were distributed from the terrace in front of the Hall by Ellen

Sophia Christy, the bridegroom's sister.

After further refreshment, followed by exercise and amusements on the 'bright green turf', all the people gathered on the side of the hill to watch a display of fireworks given by Brock & Co. of the Crystal Palace. The display included a very special piece – a huge wheel illuminating the words 'Bramall – Kircassock' with the monogram of the bride and bridegroom in the centre.

Immediately after the fireworks the return journey to Stockport commenced, 'the party momentarily stopping at the Park gates to admire a large Brunswick star in gas on the triumphal arch, and then continuing the walk singing merrily most of the way, in the exuberance of their spirits at having been so munificently entertained by their employer'.[4]

The massive staff of workers and helpers required to make possible the festivities of this tremendous day can only be imagined. The *County News* report paid special tribute to the committee who marshalled and managed the procession, the foreman of the carpenters who supervised the erection of the great tent, the waterproof sheet manufacturer who supplied the canvas for the various tents and the large marquee, the staff of one hundred and fifty waiters, the Superintendent of Police, and many others. The paper also felt sure its readers would be interested to know something about the bill of fare. The 2120 people consumed 'in addition to the three oxen, the mutton and the lamb, and the 200 plum puddings, to which reference has already been made' – 150 rabbit pies, 657 gallons of ale and porter, 20 gallons of sherry, 3500 bottles of ginger beer and lemonade, 4 gallons of cordials, 400 pounds in weight of sweets, 216 quarts of milk (for tea), plus 'the many other concomitants of a well-furnished table, all of which were equally abundant in quantity and excellent in quality'.

The detailed accounts kept by Wakefield Christy show that the personal cost to him for this great fête was £358 9s. 2d. The firm of Christy & Co. added a further £276 12s. 10d. to cover the cost of buildings and amusements, making a total expenditure of £635 2s. 0d.

Two children were born to Mr and Mrs Wakefield Christy at Bramall Hall. Their eldest son, Sydney Richardson – the 'little one' for whom the fourth cheer had been given – was indeed born the year following the wedding, and a daughter, Edith Mary, was born in 1875. Their youngest son, Geoffry, was born five years after they had left Bramhall; this son (later Sir Geoffry Christie-Miller) and his son (Lt-Col. John Christie-Miller) were to become in turn the twentieth-century managers of the firm of Christy & Co., hatters, in Stockport.[5]

In the summer of 1876 the Christy lease of Bramall Hall expired and, after seventeen years' residence in Stockport, Wakefield Christy returned to London. In that year, also, John William Handley Davenport attained his twenty-fifth birthday.

Chapter 6   JOHN WILLIAM HANDLEY DAVENPORT AND
             THE SALE

On 24 October 1876 the manor and lands of Bramhall were legally conveyed to John William Handley Davenport as directed in his father's will. Two days later he married, at St Jude's Church, Kensington, Fanny Constance Mabel Broadwood, youngest daughter of John Jervis Broadwood of Buchan Hill, Sussex, and a member of the family famous for their 'Broadwood pianos'.

The newly-married couple could have resided at Bramall Hall for only a few months, at the most, for on 24 January 1877 came the news that John William Handley Davenport had arranged to sell the estate. The *Manchester Courier* was the first to make the announcement. 'The fine old mansion of Bramhall Hall . . . has been sold, we understand, to a building company, no doubt with the view of converting the domain into sites for villa residences'. A description of the Hall followed, and then the further information, 'We are informed that something like £200,000 has been paid for the hall and estate by the company who have secured it'. The announcement that sale had actually taken place was premature, but the facts were substantially correct. The contract of sale was signed by J. W. H. Davenport on 12 March 1877, and conveyance to the purchasers – the Freeholders Company Limited – was made in August 1877. This company, which had its head office in Cross Street, Manchester, had been formed only in 1876, with the main object of acquiring lands and buildings for development or resale.

On Monday, Tuesday, Wednesday and Thursday, 7-10 May 1877, a great sale of Davenport furniture took place. Bramall Hall was open for viewing on the last two days of the previous week, and a catalogue, showing the 909 lots into which the furniture had been divided, could be bought for one shilling. Newspaper articles described the interior of the building room by room, commenting on the long history of the Davenport family and deploring the forthcoming sale. 'Antiquarians and lovers of ancient art will learn with regret that the contents of Bramhall Hall, in Cheshire, are next week to be disposed of by public auction', wrote the

Manchester Courier on 2 May. The *Manchester Weekly Times* considered it 'almost to be an act of vandalism that it [the building] should be separated from the treasures which it contains', and the *Cheshire County News* declared that 'the announcement [of sale] is calculated to produce a feeling of regret to thousands in this neighbourhood who regard this historical hall with an interest far beyond that excited by the more modern mansions of the merchant princes which stud the environs of Cottonopolis.' 'From Stockport to Bramhall Hall is a favourite walk of the toilers in mills and factories and workshops', continued the latter paper. 'Within a comparatively short distance they find themselves in the midst of hedgerows and green fields, the carol of birds and the cawing of rooks, and can inhale a purer air than that smoky mixture which at times half-stifles the dwellers in the town.'[1]

Contemporary accounts of the sale show that many people took advantage of the opportunity of a free view of the interior of the Hall before it was stripped of its furniture. 'The scene which Bramhall Hall has presented during the past week, on the several days of the sale, has been disagreeable and incongruous – very animated and very sad', reported the *Manchester City News*. The weather had been good and it brought out, besides the brokers and the buyers, 'old ladies who can no more resist an auction than a moth can resist a candle, and a large number of that nondescript class, of both sexes, who seem to make it their business to go wherever there is likely to be an assemblage and nothing to pay'. There was 'a string of hansom cabs and spring carts' outside the Hall gates, but inside, 'in spite of the crowd, the rooms seemed empty; in spite of the holiday-making, it was impossible to resist a feeling of melancholy'. Similar sentiments were expressed in *The Athenæum*. 'Another historic hall has, alas, had to succumb to circumstances, and is now a thing of the past . . . The family pictures, plate and papers, with some of the old armour and oak carvings, have been retained by the late owner, but it has grieved the hearts of many people to see other old family relics, which should have been preserved, scattered in all directions.'[2]

The *Manchester Courier* printed a day-by-day description of the main lots offered, with the prices fetched and the surnames of the purchasers.[3] The first day's sale concentrated on the upstairs rooms. In the upper banqueting hall a fine bordered Turkey carpet was sold to 'Adams', ten chippendale chairs went for £5 each to 'Robinson', and a large sideboard on massive hewn oak supports for £38 to 'Ford'. In the chapel room (or state bedroom) a fine old bedstead with four carved figures of the Apostles on the headboard fetched £100 and a magnificent antique oak cabinet £85. There was some spirited bidding for the old snaffle bridles and other Cromwellian relics in the plaster room, though it is interesting to note that Alfred Burton, writing some ten years later, was a little cynical about the true pedigree of some of these articles. According to Burton, both Sir Salusbury and Colonel Davenport had been keen collectors, 'sparing no efforts to acquire any old piece when they saw it', and much of the old oak furniture at Bramall Hall – and some of the armour and other trappings supposedly left by Cromwell's soldiers – 'had, therefore, but a passing glance at the old place'.[4] Whatever the truth of this statement, the most important item in the plaster room – the heraldic tapestry – was a genuine Davenport treasure. Yet concerning the tapestry the *Manchester Courier* commented, 'it is evident that it was formerly hung upon the wall as a decorative feature of the room, but it has now been degraded to serve the office of a floor-carpet'. 'It is probably the finest piece of heraldic tapestry in the kingdom, and yet no Davenport had public spirit enough to buy it', wrote *The Athenæum*.[5] The tapestry was sold for only £25, and the name of the purchaser was 'Christy'. Stephen Christy, who had once lived with his brother at Bramall Hall, was now furnishing his own home in Stockport, and his name featured several times as a purchaser of important items of furniture.

On the second day of the sale the paradise room and withdrawing room were among those cleared. *The Athenæum* reported, 'A bed with hangings of curiously worked needlework, depicting Adam and Eve in Paradise and the Fall of Man . . . has , we believe, found a home in another of the great Davenport houses, and was purchased for £150 by Mr Bromley Davenport, of Capesthorne, M.P.'[6] In the withdrawing room a magnificent axminster carpet 26 ft by 18 ft 'in condition equal to new' fetched £29, a rare old Japanese cabinet £13 1s. 0d., ten walnutwood chairs £5 5s. 0d. each, and an old oak arm chair, with carved panels representing a boar hunt and bull baiting, £29 8s. 0d. A magnificent seventeenth-century Italian cabinet, profusely decorated and signed *Carlos Jacop f*, with numerous drawers, cupboards and inner drawers, was thought to have been sold for 210 guineas, but was later withdrawn from the sale because the desired reserve had not been reached.[7] 'Christy' bought 'a full trichord grand pianoforte . . . by Collard and Collard, in handsome rosewood case' (£64), and a double-action harp went to another purchaser.

The third day's sale saw the garden and outside equipment and the plants in the vinery and fernery disposed of first. The rooms on the ground floor were then cleared. A Chubb warranted fraud-proof wrought-iron safe in the housekeeper's room went to 'Ford' (one of the biggest buyers in the sale) for £60, as did also the antique oak sideboard in the great hall (£26) and the full-size billiard table by Thurston (£82) in the room now called the lower banqueting hall. Two curious life-size figures, carved out of wood and painted, were sold for 75s. Apparently they stood one on each side of the sideboard in the great hall where they could hardly fail to attract attention. A visitor on a sight-seeing tour of Bramall Hall one hundred years earlier has thus described them: 'a carving in Profile as large as the life of an old Beggar Woman in the neighbourhood of Bramall with a Pair of Clogs on & a pipe in her mouth & painted to a striking likeness as they told us of the original she is in a posture of dancing to the tune of a Wooden legd Fidler compos'd of the like materials with herself'.[8]

The fourth and final day of the sale was concerned almost entirely with the contents of the library. The books were divided into 175 lots, and included a copy of Ogilby's *Britannia* (1675) among other rare works, four bundles of old school books, some naval and military works, and a complete set of Marshall's *Royal Naval Biography*, wherein was an account of the early naval career of Captain Salusbury Pryce Humphreys.

The most valuable item which the library – and indeed the whole house – possessed, had changed hands before the sale began. It was a splendid manuscript Bible of about the late 14th or early 15th century. The *Manchester Weekly Times* described it as 'one of the most valuable books known to English collectors . . . written in double columns, and bound in old red morocco'. Inside the Bible were the following inscriptions: 'I leave this as a heirloom to the rightful heirs of Bramhall', and 'I, Sir Henry Saynor, priest, read this book through in 26 days – 1576-7'.[9] This must have been the Bible which so impressed Barritt on his visit to Bramall Hall in the summer of 1777. He said he had seen it in the same room as the Paradise Bed, and he called it 'a Folio manuscript Bible in old English . . . the leaves . . . was Vellum . . . the Bible cover d with leather'. Barritt added that he could find no date in the book 'but observ'd to be wrote on the inside of the Bible sealing that it was took as an Heriot from one of the name of Davenport & read in at the Buriall of one of the Davenports of Bramall about 80 years ago'.[10] This manuscript Bible was sold privately for £1000.

The local newspapers agreed in lamenting the break-up of a historic mansion house, but they were uniformly silent as to the real reason for the sale. The standards of taste in reporting, combined with the status of the vendor, ensured that a veil was drawn over this aspect of the sale. 'However much one may marvel at the voluntary abandonment of a house so old and so honourable', wrote the *Manchester City News*, 'this unusual lack of sentiment and pride of race are not subjects for public comment. We are simply concerned with the unhappy fact that one of the oldest and best-preserved of English houses has been broken up, and that its removal is a distinct loss to us both as a source of actual knowledge of the past and a source of noble inspiration in the present. There is nothing so absolutely irrecoverable as such a place as Bramhall was, before possession was given up to the auctioneer'. This paper came nearer than any other to a direct condemnation of the action of John William Handley Davenport, for, after a brief reference to a derogatory legend concerning the origin of the felon's head crest of the Davenport family, the article concluded:

> An auctioneer's hammer might now fitly be added to the quarterings of the present representative of this ancient line. [11]

Ten years later, in the privacy of his manuscript *History of Bramhall*, Alfred Burton was even more specific. He wrote:

> He [John William Handley Davenport] could not say with Lord Chief Justice Crew (in the case of the Earldom of Oxford): 'I suppose that there is no man that hath any apprehension of gentry or nobleness, but his affection stands to the continuance of so noble a name or fame, and would take hold of a twig or a twine thread to uphold it'.

Then Burton added his own comment.

> And although Dr Johnson once observed to a young lord, boasting of a long line of ancestors, 'A wise man never attempts to trace his genealogy too far back, because if he do, he is sure to run upon an ancestor who has been hanged', one would have thought that an ancestry of seven centuries would engender some little feeling of respect and affection for the old name. [12]

It was left to Burton, too, to suggest a specific reason for the sale, apart from the general factor of financial difficulties. Local rumour must have given him cause for this note concerning John William Handley Davenport:

> It is said that the reason he disposed of the estate was that his wife did not like the place. [13]

On the night of 26 July 1877, one week before the conveyance was signed, the three coffins containing the remains of Martha, William

Davenport and William Davenport Davenport were removed from the vault in Bramall Hall chapel. It was an eerie occasion, as Alfred Burton discovered when he questioned the official of the Stockport Cemetery who had superintended the work. The vault was opened late at night, the only lighting being by candles. It was 16 ft deep, built of brick and coped with stone, and the bottom was of sand. The coffin of William Davenport (which would be the second to be raised) was enclosed in another coffin of lead, and it was necessary to bind it with rope before the men could venture to lift it. The third coffin, which must have been that of Martha (though, Burton was told, there was no coffin plate to identify her), had gone completely rotten, leaving the skeleton revealed, and the cemetery superintendent commented on the exceptional length of her skull and face, 'very narrow, and most extraordinary long'. 'I never saw one so long', Burton reported him as saying, 'and I have seen hundreds'. This coffin would be at the bottom of the vault and an embarrassing incident occurred while it was being raised. When the ladder had been put down the vault the three men on the job saw a bright light on the woman's body which they were convinced was a diamond. But neither of the two who descended the ladder could find the diamond – if such it was – and each became suspicious that the other had taken it. Later reflection had convinced the man in charge that if the light had indeed come from a diamond, the stone had been lost. He agreed that the admission of air to the rotten wood might, possibly, have caused some kind of phosphorescent light, but insisted (to Burton) that the light was too bright, 'as it sent off rays like a star'.[14]

The coffins were re-interred in Cheadle Hulme graveyard and the stone, previously over the vault, was put over the new grave. The vault in Bramall Hall chapel was then completely filled in.

On 3 August 1877 the Bramhall estate of the Davenport family (a total of 1918 acres) passed to the Freeholders Company for £200,000 and the following day the company mortgaged the manor and premises to John William Handley Davenport for £100,000. The amount was repayable in four annual instalments, plus interest, and the arrangement seems to have been a device for giving the company time to pay the second half of its debt. Instalments due in 1878 and 1879 were duly paid, but thereafter the company became behindhand with the repayments. In documents relating to this agreement John William Handley Davenport is described as 'of Kensington, Middlesex'. By 1881 he had settled at Clipsham Hall, in Rutland, having inherited this estate from his maternal uncle, John Handley, of Newark.

John Handley's will was made in 1879 – two years after the sale of the Bramhall estate – and it imposed strict conditions on his nephew. The Clipsham property was entailed, and there was legal obligation for the tenant-for-life to take and use the surname and arms of 'Handley' in addition to his own surname and arms. Three months after his bachelor uncle's death in December 1880 the new squire of Clipsham assumed by Royal Licence the additional surname of 'Handley', becoming known as J. W. H. Davenport-Handley.

Thereafter the qualities and drive typical of a squire of Bramhall were transferred to his new estate. His private life, however, was not without tragedy. In 1885 he divorced his wife for adultery, a procedure so expensive as to be prohibitive to all but the wealthy, and still so rare as to be undertaken in only the gravest cases. His ex-wife immediately remarried; it was nearly three years before J. W. H. Davenport-Handley, who now had the sole custody of two young sons, himself married for the second time. In 1910, when he was in his sixtieth year, a second Royal Licence gave to J. W. H. Davenport-Handley authority to take and use the surname of 'Humphreys' (his paternal grandfather's family name) in addition to the names he already used, and to quarter the arms of 'Humphreys' with the arms of 'Davenport' and 'Handley'.

John William Handley Davenport-Handley-Humphreys died on 27 July 1914 and was buried in the quiet country churchyard of Clipsham. 'Although he was not closely identified with official life, he held various public offices', wrote the *Stamford Mercury*, thereby indicating both the aloofness of the man who had so harshly severed the ties binding him to the past and the typical characteristics of service which made him a true son of the landed gentry. 'As a generous landlord and a true friend to the poor, not only of the immediate neighbourhood but of the whole county, he will be truly missed'.[15]

Perhaps the young man, John William Handley Davenport, was not so entirely devoid of family feeling as people such as Alfred Burton supposed. He was responsible for the dispersal of many costly and beautiful family treasures, but he took to his new home some of the more intimate and personal possessions, some of which remain to this day. In addition to the family portraits there are various pieces of wood carving, including the Jacobean overmantel bearing the names of Sir William and Dame Dorothy Davenport, which once stood over the fireplace in the great hall at Bramhall. There is the seventeenth-century oak cradle which has rocked generations of Davenport children from the time of the seventh

William Davenport, and there is the magnificent Italian cabinet made by Carlos Jacop which was withdrawn from sale in 1877. Among the books which remain at Clipsham several have newspaper cuttings relating to members of the Davenport family pasted on to the fly-leaves. There is one, one only, of the chained prayer books from Bramall Hall chapel – the personal prayer book of 'J. W. H. Davenport'. There is a Book of Common Prayer of the time of George I, obviously intended for the reading desk of the chapel and, from the wear and tear of its pages, very heavily used for Evening Prayer. An insert paper, handwritten with new names of the Royal Family, shows that the book was still used during the time of George III. There is a Bible inscribed 'The gift of Salusbury Pryce Humphreys to his Wife Maria', and later 'Now Maria Davenport to her son W: D: Davenport', and written on two blank leaves at the end are the dates of birth and marriage of Colonel Davenport and details of his children, concluding with

> John William Handley born 19 Octr
> 1851 & baptized in Bramall Hall Chapel –
> God Fathers John Handley Esq & John Handley
> Esq. junr his Grand Father and Uncle –
> God Mother Lady Davenport.

And would it be a flight of fancy to suppose that a small 'Church Service', a Prayer Book and Bible printed as one, bound in very thin leather and with the Davenport bookplate inside the cover, was a gift to the last Davenport of Bramhall from his godmother on the occasion of his confirmation? The inscription, handwritten on the fly-leaf, runs:

> To my Grandson
>
>   Handley
> Jn William / Davenport   [sic]
>
> with every sincere
> blessing for his
> health & happiness
> March 18th 1866
>
> This is the best
> Book you can
> possess
>
>   Maria Davenport

Chapter 7   BRAMALL HALL – the home of Charles Nevill

For some years after the great sale of 1877 Bramall Hall stood empty. Advertisements appearing in the press show that the Freeholders Company tried to let it,[1] but no tenant appeared willing to take it over. In 1882, however, a purchaser came forward. Thomas Henry Nevill, a wealthy calico printer and owner of the Strines Printing Works, near Marple, bought Bramall Hall and the Park immediately surrounding it for his son, Charles, who was now the active head of the firm. The younger man moved to Bramhall from Mile End Hall, where he had lived since his marriage.

Bramall Hall, for so long the manorial centre of an agricultural district, now became the private residence of a man of business, a man whose family riches originated with the Industrial Revolution and whose business interests were in the cotton industry. For over thirty years Charles Henry Nevill lived at Bramall Hall. He spent large sums of money on the improvement and modernisation of the Hall and Park and in his private life he tried to identify himself with the people of the now expanding village of Bramhall.

In the 1870s, before there was any thought of his becoming 'Mr Nevill of Bramall Hall', Charles Nevill seems to have been one of a set of gay, yet fundamentally serious-minded young men who moved easily in the upper middle class world of social visits, parties and dances. He was strong-willed and impulsive, in contrast to his close friend, Henry Sidebottom, who was of a quiet disposition and a peacemaker by nature. It was through their dashing and energetic contemporary, Joseph Heape (a future Mayor of Rochdale) who was already courting Eleanor Booth, that Charles and Henry became acquainted with the daughters of Thomas Booth, cotton spinner, of Rochdale. In 1876 Henry married Fanny Elizabeth and two years later Charles Nevill married Mary Jane Booth, he being then thirty and she twenty-eight.

Very early in their married life Mary had to come to terms with the fact that her husband possessed one consuming passion which she could not share; he was an ardent fisherman. Fortunately her sense of humour and literary turn of mind helped her to cope with this situation, and she has left two highly-coloured and amusing accounts of her plight. Writing to a friend of a fishing holiday in 1879 she said:

> We have come to the end of our three days' journey into the wilderness, and reached this out-of-the-world spot at last ... If I were to give you a full, true and particular account of one day's doings it would serve as a very good example of what existence has been to your unhappy friend for the last fortnight — because tomorrow will be as today, only more so! Take my advice and never be induced to marry a man who is fond of fishing, for if you do you will wish you had never been born. [2]

Two summers later Charles and Mary were in Norway and Mary wrote with grim humour of the intensity with which her husband threw himself into his chosen occupation.

> There was a splash — a commotion — the glimpse of a vanishing tail — and then the sound as of a whole cotton mill at work as the reel whizzed round, and the salmon darted down the stream, with C[harlie] after it. Would that I had the pencil of an artist to depict that exciting chase! C.'s face was glorified, and he was so utterly oblivious of all surroundings that I might have drowned myself within five feet of him, and he would have been none the wiser ... The river, C. and the fish seemed inextricably muddled up together in one huge commotion ... After infinite patience and tact on the one hand, and infinite obstinacy on the other, the man (and the gaff) proved too much for the fish, and when I had scrambled down to the scene of the battle I found C. in an exhausted condition, embracing a salmon which, to my excited imagination, seemed to weigh about a hundred pounds. [3]

Years later when, as owner of Bramall Hall, Charles Nevill built the artificial lakes and stocked them with trout, so that he was able to indulge his chosen sport in his own park, this enjoyment of a tussle was still uppermost. 'I have got a lot of good trout this year but no 2 or 3 pounders!!!' he wrote to his young nephew, Francis Nevill Sidebottom, in the summer of 1896. 'Last night, after dinner, your Father and I went out, and I got one fish — 1 lb 6 oz — a fine fat fellow, that fought very gamely.' [4]

All his life Charles Nevill loved travel, and in his steam yacht *Victoria* he made many cruises to distant lands, collecting rare and valuable articles with which to embellish his home. On these trips he also brought back dredgings for his brother-in-law, Henry Sidebottom, who became an acknowledged authority on foraminifera. The findings of one such voyage revealed a new genus of these microscopic creatures, to which Henry

Sidebottom gave the name 'Nevillina' in honour of his friend.

Although not by training an antiquarian, Charles Nevill was intensely interested in the history and the architecture of the property which his father had acquired for him, and he aimed at preserving Bramall Hall as a historic building and not simply turning it into a desirable residence. To him must go the credit that Bramall Hall survived into the twentieth century at all. For at least the first four years of the Nevill ownership extensive repair work was being carried out to the fabric of the building itself. Here are some of the main alterations as described by Alfred Burton, the friend whose interest may have inspired Charles Nevill, and who examined every part of the building with him.

There were alterations in the great hall which revealed the original floor of this room. First 'came a flooring of flags 18 inches square and an inch and a half in thickness; then 2 inches of sand, beneath which was a flooring of red tiles 6 inches square and an inch and a half thick. Beneath this again was 2 inches of sand, placed on the top of the original white plaster floor composed of lime and sand and an inch thick – under which was the earth rammed down hard, sand and gravel.' The heating apparatus was put under the hall floor, approached from the cellar. The ceiling of the great hall was 'improved by the erection of two false beams of oak reaching from each corner of the fireplace to the west wall, over the window in the centre'.[5]

The old staircase on the south side of the building which, in Davenport days, occupied the central part of the space between the chapel and the lower banqueting hall, must have been completely taken out. According to Burton, the old stairs were by now 'nothing but a modern botch of old materials'.[6] They wound round an octagonal newel post and had oak step boards two inches thick. Nearby was a door leading almost centrally into the chapel at its west end. The elegant, new staircase was built close to the south wall and occupied all the space between chapel and banqueting hall. The central west door leading to the chapel was closed, and an older door in the north-west corner reopened.

The renovation of the chapel room (or Queen Anne room) could not have been carried out in Burton's lifetime. He described the room in 1883 with walls 'wainscoted all round with fine oak', 'a very small fireplace on the north side', and with the partition forming the anteroom still in place.[7] He makes no mention of the removal of this partition to make one large room, and the construction, in the centre of the north wall, of a large new fireplace, including on its ornate surround the bear and ragged staff which Charles Nevill chose to use as a badge. Nor does Burton mention the annexe to the south of the room, built above the chapel extension. He does, however, describe how the ornamental roof above this room was discovered.

The repairs rendered necessary in 1883 by the state of the roofs led to a singular discovery in this one. On getting into that portion over the ante-room, it was found that the principal over the west wall of the chapel room was plastered up, and a hole was made through it to gain access to the east end. The inner face of this plaster was found to be white washed and painted over with scrollwork and foliage, in black and red. In the centre of the gable were the initials and date $\begin{smallmatrix} D & K & 1 & 6 & 1 \\ W & & & & 0 \end{smallmatrix}$ supported by cherubs and surrounded by foliage – black on a white ground – on each side. The purlins and roof timbers were decorated in the same style. This plaster (formed of clay mixed with rushes and straw, and two to three inches thick) was nearly demolished through the stupidity of a workman; but the central portion was fortunately found sufficiently perfect to allow of its being placed in a frame for its preservation.

Charles Nevill and Alfred Burton had uncovered decorative work done in the time of Sir William and Dame Dorothy Davenport when the chapel room was open to the roof. Burton also draws the conclusion that 'in later times the old roof was found too draughty for modern taste, and it was counter-ceiled, the decorations being shut out.'[8]

Next, the withdrawing room, where Burton mentions particularly the work done on the fireplace and the touching up of the Elizabethan overmantel. 'The whole was formerly *whitewashed* and picked out in blue and gold', he said. 'A lintel of oak inlaid in a similar style to the doorways, and bearing the initials $\begin{smallmatrix} & N & \\ C & & M \end{smallmatrix}$ for Charles and Mary Nevill was placed over the fireplace in 1883, and the whole recoloured, which has much improved its appearance.' The withdrawing room windows could not then have been the sashed windows of William and Martha Davenport, for Burton describes them as 'in fact one vast window of 90 lights . . . divided into three rows by transoms, the glass being of a common kind'.[9]

Downstairs Charles Nevill made 'a very handsome dining room' out of the morning room, or little dining room, of Davenport days, having 'the bay window taken out, and the front, of timber, carried further east, in which is a window of 10 lights'. The library, too, according to Burton, had windows 'of modern construction' (presumably, sashed) but these were removed in 1883 and replaced by a window with lights, similar to that in the morning room.[10]

The staircase on the north must have been much altered, though few details are given. Burton called it the principal staircase, which, he said, 'leads upwards to a small bedroom on the east over the one above the morning room, and is the only part of the hall of three stories'. They called this attic bedroom the Newfoundland Room, 'but the name really appertains to the small room opening out of it on the east formed in the gable, lighted by a small window, but without fireplace'. This room, Burton claimed, had been accidentally discovered in 1840, and probably formed part of a hiding-place long since forgotten.[11]

Repair work took place in the chapel in 1883, and there was a sudden scare that the coffins removed to Cheadle Hulme churchyard in 1877 were not the only ones that lay beneath its floor. Burton records that a certain Peter Gordon, foreman in charge of the work, reported putting his chisel through the decayed wood of a coffin, 'but on perceiving what it was did not pursue his investigations further'. Work was held up for a time, but, 'Mr Nevill & I afterwards dug down to it, and found it to be a board completely decayed.' Together C. H. Nevill and Alfred Burton must have made a thorough search, for they came to the conclusion 'There are no other coffins anywhere in the chapel'.[12] The pews were not removed from the chapel at this stage for Burton mentions 'benches' on both sides of the aisle and a pew for the family on each side of the communion table. He adds that a small organ was installed by Charles Nevill in the south-west corner of the chapel, and this first organ is mentioned later as the apparent centre of ghostly activity in Bramall Hall.

Burton himself is sceptical about the existence of the Bramhall ghosts, though he devotes a substantial section of his manuscript to the various legends. He quotes in full John Leigh's poem *The Maid of Bramhall Hall*, with its story of the girl whose lover was slain by robbers in the Macclesfield forest, but first he gives his own comments on her ghost, the 'lady in white who appears to entertain an affection for the Plaster room and Paradise room'. 'Of course', he says, 'mysterious noises, especially in rough weather, are attributed to her ladyship whose identity is veiled in obscurity.' Of John Leigh's other legend of Bramall Hall – *The Red Rider* – Burton writes, 'I have not been able to identify the incident'. Another Bramall Hall ghost had a very unromantic origin. It was said to be the ghost of a servant maid who was half-murdered by one of the early Davenports in a bedroom in the north wing, and then (so Burton was told) 'dragged, screaming, to the small room in the gable in the east front (next to the "Newfoundland room") and there finished'. Of his own, and Charles Nevill's, experience of the ghosts, Burton wrote:

> I have spent many weeks in the hall; and have walked through the park at all hours of the night, but have never been gratified with a sight or sound of either of the ghosts; perhaps I have been overheard to express scepticism as to their existence, and their ghostships wont condescend to favour me with an interview . . . Mr Nevill has been more fortunate, and informs me that twice he has heard the most entrancing music proceed from an organ he had placed in the chapel. At first he thought it was his good lady, but found all the doors fastened; and it may be that the ghosts having found something unusual in the old place proceeded to find out its uses.[13]

It must have been in the course of early work in the chapel that Charles Nevill uncovered the old windows in the north wall. The discovery was mentioned in a letter written in 1888. '[I] have *uncovered* some old windows with early English mouldings which have *never* been glazed and show no signs of shutters . . .' He believed that at one time the windows had looked on to a corridor between the chapel and the great hall, and that above this corridor was a gallery, 'for I found an old doorway from [the] Chapel chamber which had been made up with wattle and daub for hundreds of years – long prior to the cutting off of the Library and plaister room from the Great Hall.'[14] He was obviously of the opinion that the mediaeval great hall was longer than the present one, extending nearer to the chapel, and the finding of the unglazed windows and the old doorway strengthened this opinion.

Charles Nevill's greatest discovery was made in the summer of 1887 in the upper banqueting hall. 'This fine room is spoiled by sham decorations' Burton wrote when making his room by room description of Bramall Hall in 1883, but over sixty years earlier Ormerod had mentioned mural paintings as one of the features of the room.[15] Their continued existence was not thought possible until work on the new staircase was in progress. Here is Burton's account of the uncovering of the murals.

> Early in June 1887, when it became necessary to strip the plaster off the west wall of the staircase, traces of colour were observed; and on taking pieces of plaster away carefully with the point of a knife, it was found that sufficient remained to give an idea of the design. Mr Nevill at once ordered the whole of the walls in this room to be stripped, which was

done with the utmost care. Thick, coarse laths, or rather ribs, had been nailed over the walls as a means of securing the plaster which was laid on them; and owing to the thickness of these laths very little of the lime plaster had come into contact with the old surface; so that, with a few spaces here and there, the paintings were found to show the' wear and tear of time only. This was extremely fortunate, as wherever the modern plaster touched the colour, the latter was totally destroyed. Immediately on being uncovered the surface was lightly brushed over with fine soft brushes, and a coating of size applied. When this was dry two coats of carriage-varnish made the whole secure from injury and remarkably clear. It was then seen that the north and east walls were painted all over with a beautiful conventionalized design of foliage, having figures of birds and animals intersperced, together with some very curious designs ... The west and south walls had been similarly treated, as shown by the remains on the wallplates and other timbers, but these sides were destroyed when the old timber walls were rebuilt, or rather partly cased with brick at the early part of the present [19th] century. Accurate drawings, carefully measured, were at once taken by Mr [name left blank] A thin coating of fine plaster or *gesso* formed the ground on which the painting was done, and it is curious to observe how the colour is clearer and more persistent on the wood than on the plaster; while in that kind of work done in 1610 ... the reverse is the case. This is due to the difference in the medium used by the painter.[16]

Charles Nevill thought that he had uncovered murals of the time of Henry VII, and 'these', he wrote, 'I am taking care to preserve'.[17] Expert opinion of today puts most of the paintings as Jacobean or late-Elizabethan, though a section on the upper part of the east wall could be of earlier date.

That Charles Nevill enjoyed his work of investigation and restoration is very obvious. Writing in 1888 to Cyril Davenport (one of the grandsons of Salusbury and Maria) he said of Bramall Hall, 'I think I know more about its probable age and construction than anyone (with the exception of one neighbour who takes a particular interest in the subject). Repairs have been endless, and in doing them I have from time to time exposed the very backbone and ribs of the house – the parts that have not been touched for hundreds of years'. Charles Nevill concluded this letter with a pointed postscript conveying not only his view of the Davenport sale, but also his delight in his own acquisition.

> P.S. That cousin of yours was a fool to part with the house – but it's an ill wind etc.[18]

When, in the spring of 1887, members of the Lancashire & Cheshire Antiquarian Society visited Bramall Hall to see the work which had been carried out, tribute was paid to the new owner. 'It was a matter for gratitude and pleasure', the mover of a vote of thanks is reported as saying, 'that such an historic pile should have fallen into the hands of Mr Nevill, whose means and taste are equal to the task of restoration and reproduction'.[19]

In the autumn of 1890 Alfred Burton died without being able to complete his account of the restoration of Bramall Hall. The previous two or three years had been devoted to work especially in the Park. Some outside work had already been necessary, and Burton records that in 1883, while work on a drain was in progress, he searched for the foundations of the gatehouse side of the Hall, which had been pulled down one hundred years earlier. 'Although I carefully examined the ground no traces of any foundations were visible'. He then realised that the Hall had been built without 'foundations' in the modern sense; the timber and stone rested directly on the soil. That same year, 1883, a small shippon and stable which still remained to the west of the gatehouse side were demolished, and the timber and grey stone slates used in repair of the Hall. In their place, a Victorian stable and coach-house were erected.[20]

The most important recorded outside work was the building of the 'new road' in the spring and summer of 1888. This was, in effect, a diversion of the old drive, which was taken well away from the house so that it passed at some distance from the chapel at the south side. It made the slope of the hill easier for the horse traffic of the day, and it also made the house more private. Any tradition that the public might have a right to a road running directly up to Bramall Hall was firmly overruled by its new owner.

Burton recorded in diary form the early work on the road.

> 1888. April 5. The chestnut tree at the north end of the row cut down for the new road . . .
> 1888. April 14. The widening of the brook above the weir, and the planting of the mound on the north side completed. The new road to the south of the present one staked out from the east lodge to the top of the brow near the chapel, and the pillars of the bridge over the Carr brook commenced.[21]

The activity of road-making must have produced some interested sightseers, as well as giving employment to a number of people. It was at this time that Charles Nevill complained of damage to the two great felons' heads over the south gateposts, writing in characteristic vein to the *Cheshire County News* that he intended 'to find for them a safe resting place, where passing fools can do them no injury'. Later that summer, when work on the road was well advanced, an onlooker, Sam Bardsley, wrote a dialect poem entitled *A Ramble reaund Bramha Park*, describing the work he witnessed there. The very best in equipment was obviously being provided, for

> They'n waggons theer for t'shift their stuff, –
> These too are wonderful enough;
> For aw cud see from wheer aw stud,
> They run on metals made of wood.

The poet knew some of the men working on the job, and he watched them tipping and levelling the site.

> There's Shirky, Barrell, Skamer and Bill,
> Their duty is these waggons t'fill;
> Then to th' tip its taen by Merry Legs,
> An level't bi a mon cawd Peg. [22]

The diversion of the road to the south of the Hall made the old east front entrance into a private doorway leading to the garden. Here Charles Nevill laid out terraces, setting the felons' heads, one each side, at the top of the steps. He diverted the course of the Ladybrook at the foot of the hill so that it was possible to construct the artificial lakes on the north side. And at some date (not mentioned by Burton) Charles Nevill renewed the roof of the Hall itself, adding gables and reconstructing the brick chimney stacks in Tudor style. The suspension of the group of small gables on the west – a method of construction designed to take the weight off the bay window beneath – was found especially interesting by the Surveyor to the Hazel Grove & Bramhall Urban District Council when he examined the building about 1940.

The East Lodge (built before the work on the 'new road' was started) and its counterpart at the west end of the grounds are both late-nineteenth-century in date, although half-timbered and built in 'black and white' style. The East Lodge housed the head gardener, and the West Lodge, the coachman. The Hall Cottage, a roughcast building which was far more than a cottage in the accepted sense, was built in 1895 near the West Lodge

Bramall Hall in Davenport days: east front showing direction of drive before alteration

Bramall Hall in Davenport days: west front c.1860

3 Bromale shield with woodcarving under the oriel window in the courtyard

4 Sir William Davenport

5 Dame Dorothy Davenport

6 Paradise Bed: part of
canopy showing
embroidery and
lettering

*The great hall in Davenport days
showing old fireplace with
woodcarving above*

8 West end of the chapel in Davenport
days: the black lettering of the
Commandments is complete

9   *Sir Salusbury Davenport*   10   *Maria Davenport*

11   *Invitation card for Wakefield Christy's wedding festivities*

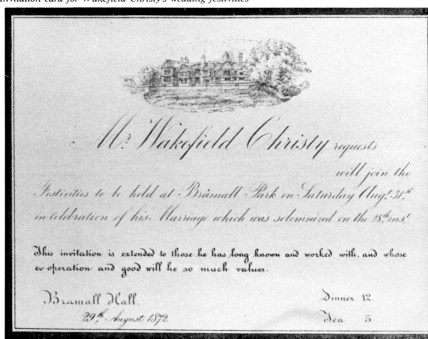

12   *West front of Bramall Hall showing gables added by C. H. Nevill*

13   *Charles Henry Nevill*

14   *Mary Nevill*

15   *Withdrawing room as furnished by C. H. Nevill*

16   *John Henry Davies*

17   *Amy Davies*

8 *West end of the chapel as found by the Hazel Grove & Bramhall Urban District Council: the black lettering of the Commandments has flaked, revealing the mural painting beneath*

9 *Inscriptions in the Bible returned by C. H. Wrigley to Bramall Hall: it had been given to him to commemorate the restoration of the chapel*

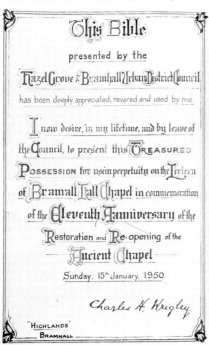

This Bible

presented by the

Hazel Grove & Bramhall Urban District Council

has been deeply appreciated, revered and used by me.

I now desire, in my lifetime, and by leave of the Council, to present this TREASURED POSSESSION for use in perpetuity on the Lectern of Bramall Hall Chapel in commemoration of the Eleventh Anniversary of the Restoration and Re-opening of the Ancient Chapel

Sunday. 15th January. 1950.

Charles H. Wrigley

"HIGHLANDS"
BRAMHALL

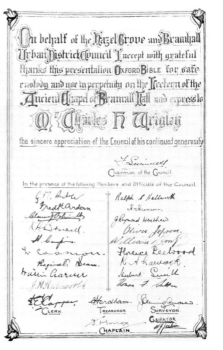

On behalf of the Hazel Grove and Bramhall Urban District Council I accept with grateful thanks this presentation OXFORD BIBLE for safe custody and use in perpetuity on the Lectern of the Ancient Chapel of Bramall Hall and express to

Mr Charles H Wrigley

the sincere appreciation of the Council of his continued generosity

Chairman of the Council.

In the presence of the following Members and Officials of the Council.

CLERK   TREASURER   SURVEYOR
CHAPLAIN   CURATOR

20   Davenport family portraits being inspected by David and Leslie Davenport-Handley (left of centre) with the civic party, 20 May 1950: the portraits on the extreme right are of William and Martha Davenport

21   Portion of the Davenport Pedigree Roll displayed by Reginald Dean: note the felon's head crest

and became the home of Henry and Fanny Sidebottom.

In the autumn of 1890 Kate Douglas Wiggin, the American authoress, first visited Bramall Hall, and she has left behind a description of the building and its occupants which, seen from the point of view of a 'daughter of a youthful nation', is both amusing and refreshing. Kate was at this time a young widow, already well known for her best-selling stories for, and about, children. The occasion of her visit was a holiday voyage to Europe which, by the kindness of friends, she was enabled to make shortly after her first husband's death. She travelled extensively in England and on the Continent and then decided on another quick visit to London before her return to the United States. Here she found an invitation awaiting her from Mr and Mrs Charles Nevill of Bramall Hall.

> I had met them at a London dinner earlier in the season, and there had been a decided friendliness between us from the first. I knew that Mr Nevill was a wealthy business man in Manchester, but he was something entirely different in manner, in temperament, in tastes and proclivities from any other man of business I had ever met in England. That his father had built up the great manufactory and bequeathed it to his only son may have accounted for the fact that the son traveled about the world incessantly, collecting rare things from every country he visited and living a life of leisure, devoted to books and art . . .

> I little thought, when I first beheld Bramall in all its picturesque beauty and grandeur, that it would become a sort of English home to me, revisited every year for more than twenty years, until first the lovely mistress, and then the clever and brilliant master, died and left a great blank in my list of English friendships . . .

> After my marriage to Mr Riggs, in 1895, he, as well as my sister, were welcomed into the heart of the family circle.[23]

In the excitement of her first arrival, Kate Douglas Wiggin wrote an enthusiastic letter home to her unmarried sister, Nora Archibald Smith. 'Behold me in the lap of luxury!' Kate wrote. 'Behold me, the daughter of a youthful nation, disporting myself on an Elizabethan-and-Norman background!' Nora kept the letter, and years later Kate included it in her autobiography.

> I have written you of the Nevills of Bramall Hall, but I can hardly bear to describe my surroundings when I remember that you and mother

are living in a San Francisco 'flat', and who am I, pray, that I should be
dwelling in a house the newest portion of which dates from Queen
Elizabeth's time . . . With its jeweled windows, its green terraces where
peacocks flaunt their tails, its hedges of yew and holly and its own trout
stream; with its armor, its tapestries, its silver and carved oak, it is a
perfect example of the ideal English country house.

Part of it is several hundred years old . . . but my host reminds me
daily that other parts of Bramall were built when America was being
discovered! He has been restoring the place steadily during the seven
years of his ownership and the workmen are still on the premises, for he
is doing everything with rare taste and devoting hours of study every day
that the result may approach perfection. They are restoring the private
chapel now (under the same roof, you know, on the ground floor) and I
steal in for a moment now and then to sit in one of the ancient pews and
lift one of the precious old prayer books chained to the oaken rail. I
asked Mr Nevill the reason of this ancient custom, and he replied
exasperatingly that American tourists sometimes visit the chapel, but I
am confident that there is a pleasanter explanation than this.

There is everything here we ever read about in a Disraeli novel. The
great hall, its walls covered with arms and armor and its stained-glass
windows emblazoned with colored coats of arms, has a fireplace large
enough for two beautiful carved stone benches in the chimney, where we
sit after dinner or at tea-time. The furnishing is of course entirely of
antique pieces and altogether superb, while the bronze and lacquers and
ivories and porcelains reflect the firelight and intoxicate me with their
beauty. Oh! my dears, if only you could see that hall lighted by candles
at five o'clock, the men in their shooting clothes, Mrs Nevill with her
train brocaded with red Venetian flowers (all her dresses match the
house), the beautiful tea equipage, crumpets, hot muffins, marmalade and
pâté-de-foie-gras sandwiches, servants in livery, *and* a great gray boar-
hound on the rug in front of the fire – I cannot go on, my hand trembles
with excitement!

Later Kate added a further instalment.

Upstairs each guest's name is written on a card enclosed in a frame
on the door (I am going to put mine on my hotel sitting-room door in
New York! it is the only inexpensive feature of the establishment that I
can find to imitate!) My room is at least thirty feet square. A mullioned
window twelve feet long and four feet high, all leaded panes of glass,
looks on the park, the terraces, and the little river that flows through the
park. The walls and ceilings are paneled oak and my bed is seven feet
wide. When I go to bed at night there is a procession of room-maids,

ladies' maids, housekeepers and others, with warming pans, jugs of hot water, candles, eider-down quilts, and hot gin and water! In the morning a procession arrives with different articles, and oh! how I like it . . .

This afternoon Mr Nevill took me through the entire house . . . explaining the nature of all his wonderful treasures, which are so arranged that, notwithstanding their value and rarity, and their extraordinary number, the effect is somehow kept from being that of a museum . . . There are many stairways, added, no doubt, at various periods, and the very afternoon of my arrival when I left the Davenport room (my bedroom) for the great hall at tea-time – wandering along what I believed to be the right path, but a good deal occupied with the effect of my new white tea gown [she had booked a cheaper passage home than intended, in order to have the gown made for the occasion] – I opened and threw back a heavy oak doorway and confronted, somewhat theatrically, the housekeeper's sitting-room where six maids, a valet, and a coachman were having their tea.

'I'm awfully sorry!' I said. 'I have lost my way. Will you kindly show me the hall?'

They did so, thinking little of my mentality or sense of direction, I fancy, but the lady's-maid told me that the housemaid said that the valet told her that the coachman remarked that 'first 'e thought it was a h'angel standing in the dark doorway.'

A later letter written from Bramall Hall is also included in Kate Douglas Wiggin's autobiography. This letter was addressed to her mother and concerned almost entirely with the cooking and bills-of-fare provided at Bramall Hall for guests. The style is more consciously clever and the letter 'extra-well composed', as the authoress herself admits, for it was intended to be sent the round of her family in America. 'The English can make bread sauce suitable for a king, while ours is only fit for poultices', Kate wrote, and there is much more in the same vein. The paragraph describing the kitchens at Bramall Hall is interesting:

I sometimes steal a half-hour at tea-time, or just before luncheon, to collogue with the Scotch artist who presides over the Bramall kitchens, just to watch her combine the articles that her docile assistant has gathered on the table to await her skillful hand. From the wonderful old leaded glass windows of the kitchen I can see the velvety green terraces, the shining trout-stream, and the avenues bordered with blooming rhododendrons, while within all is peace. In the range burns a bright fire, the copper cooking-utensils gleam on the wall, the table and floor are white as snow, and there are yellow bowls and old British luster saucers, with here and there on the great table dabs of green butter colored with spinach, hillocks of whipped cream, slices of red tomato and hard-boiled egg, snippets of scarlet pepper and minced olives, and little heaps of silver anchovies, all waiting to be made into savories.

Perhaps it was to this very same 'Scotch artist' (otherwise the cook-housekeeper) that Kate Douglas Wiggin gave a copy of her book *Timothy's Quest*, with the inscription:

> From Mrs Riggs, a fair Book-Cook to Miss — a Perfect British Cook-Book [24]

The name of the recipient is omitted in Nora Archibald Smith's collection of biographical fragments, but it was a member of the staff at Bramall Hall.

Although Kate Douglas Wiggin is now remembered for only one book, *Rebecca of Sunnybrook Farm*, her other stories were also tremendously popular in her own day, and none more so in Britain than her three volumes of *Penelope's Experiences*, a work which was begun at Bramall Hall. Stimulated, no doubt, by the waggishness of her host, the first part of *Penelope's Experiences in England*, which describes the society life of three American girls in London, was written while the author was a guest of the Nevills at Bramhall.

In politics Charles Nevill was a staunch Conservative, and much of his effort within the local community was given to the support of the Tory party. He was an enthusiastic member of the Primrose League, an organisation founded in honour of the great Benjamin Disraeli, and politics brought him into close association with Coningsby Disraeli, nephew of the statesman and Conservative M.P. for Altrincham, in which constituency Bramhall was then included. Illness, and the death of his wife in 1901, caused Charles Nevill to retire from politics for several years, but he seems to have been jerked back to public life by the overwhelming defeat of the Conservative party in 1906, when Coningsby Disraeli (among others) lost his seat in the landslide to the Liberals. Charles Nevill became one of the strongest supporters of the Tariff Reform movement in the country and, to the time of his death, an active and vigorous worker for the Conservative party.

Locally, Charles Nevill failed to see a Conservative member elected for Bramhall in the first county council elections of 1889, but he himself was returned unopposed as the Conservative member for the Marple division of Cheshire. He thus became one of the first members of the newly formed Cheshire County Council, holding the seat until 1894 when illness caused his resignation. During the last decade of the nineteenth century he took a prominent part in the movement for a Bramhall Urban District, giving evidence at the hearing on 3 July 1896.[25] This application was rejected, but a similar petition made four years later led to the formation, from the five townships of Bosden, Bramhall, Norbury, Offerton and Torkington, of the Urban District of Hazel Grove-cum-Bramhall.

In 1888 there was also a movement to provide a mission church for Bramhall and here, too, Charles Nevill was in the forefront. He attended the first meeting to consider ways of reintroducing Anglican services to Bramhall, and he gave generous monetary support to the mission church, which opened in October 1890. He also allowed the church free and regular use of the 'village hall', an iron hut which he had put up at his own expense in order to encourage community life in Bramhall. Yet his benefactions to the church outside contrast strangely with his apparent neglect of that ancient place of worship in his own home – the chapel at Bramall Hall. In all Charles Nevill's years at Bramhall no restoration there was accomplished.

At some time in his life Charles Nevill contracted a hip disease and became lame in one leg; thereafter he walked only with the aid of crutches. The disability does not seem to have detracted from the powerful impact his personality made on other people; in some ways it may even have enhanced it. Years later his niece, Katharine Sidebottom, thus remembered her uncle:

> He was a great character. Very strong-willed, decisive and clever in many ways, and very good with children, so that (though I would never have dreamed of disobeying him) I was never afraid of him.
>
> His big chair was on the right of the hall fire and he sat there with his game leg on a stool while I sat on him, and he would go through 'I was a farmer, a farmer's boy' with all appropriate noises, while my aunt at her writing-table would protest 'Oh, Charlie, do be quiet!' But he would only proceed with great gusto to my infinite pleasure.[26]

There are other instances on record of the inflexible determination of which Charles Nevill's niece speaks, and they show him as a stern upholder of his rights. He would allow no bicycle – either ridden or wheeled – on his 'new road', and there were notices to this effect on the gates at each end. He persuaded the Parish Council to allow him to close a footpath which had by now come to be regarded as a right of way, and in 1896 a poaching incident ended in a public statement concerning Mr Nevill's fishing rights in the Ladybrook. This incident involved a member of the local police force, though the fact was not made public at the time. Here is Charles Nevill's account of the affair, taken from a letter to his nephew, Francis.

> We have been looking out for poachers lately and 10 days ago we caught one of the Hazel Grove policemen and another man, netting at 3 o'clock one Sunday morning. The policeman was 'removed' by the Chief Constable at once to another place, and I hear he has had 4/– a week taken off his wages, so he has paid dearly for his fishing. The other man I let off with an apology in the papers, as he had only gone as the [policeman's] friend. [27]

The apology appeared in the *Stockport Advertiser* of 3 July 1896, and immediately below came a warning, signed by Chas H. Nevill.

> IT HAVING COME TO MY KNOWLEDGE that certain Persons have been FISHING and POACHING IN THE LADY BROOK, and also that certain other persons have been illegally granting permission to fish, I HEREBY GIVE NOTICE that no person may fish in those parts of the Lady Brook which belong to Lord Newton, or to the Freeholders Co., or to myself, without my permission in writing ... No gamekeeper, caretaker, or tenant has power to grant permission; and I further give notice that should any one, after this date, be found fishing in the said stream, no apology or excuse will be accepted, but the offender will be prosecuted according to the law.

According to the recollections of the Sidebottom children it was the old gamekeeper who, with their uncle, lay in ambush by the Ladybrook until three o'clock that summer Sunday morning, and caught the village policeman at his shady work. The Nevills had no children of their own and the Sidebottom children became the 'children of the Hall'. 'I ran wild all over the grounds', Katharine Sidebottom wrote of her own childhood. 'Some of the happiest hours of my life were spent swinging in the old orchard under the apple-blossom ... and in the wild wood where I played Robin Hood all alone, or Roderick Dhu among the bracken.' [28]

It had been the hope of Thomas Nevill when he bought Bramall Hall for his son, Charles, that the place would remain in the Nevill family, for a trust made immediately after purchase arranged for future Nevill succession. Should Charles Nevill have no children to whom to leave the property he was required to nominate one of the children of his married sister, Maria Eliza Stiff, to succeed him. So it came about that Thomas Stiff, the eldest of the nephews, came as a young man to live at Bramall Hall, taking his uncle's name and becoming associated with him in business, in public life and in the management of the estate.

When War came in 1914 Charles Nevill is said to have offered Bramall Hall as a hospital for wounded soldiers, but his offer was not accepted. 'He lent his powerful financial and personal help to providing hospital accommodation elsewhere'.[29] During the last two years of his life he threw himself wholeheartedly into the munitions production of the St Helens Smelting Works, a firm he had founded, seeing this as his best contribution to the British war effort. But throughout the country he was becoming known in a different way. Thousands of people read in their *Daily Express* of the generosity and continuous contributions of an unknown benefactor to the 'Cheery Fund' which the paper was organising on behalf of the men at the front. This benefactor adopted the pseudonym of 'Diogenes', the philosopher who, legend asserted, laid down so austere a rule of life for himself that he lived in a tub. He sent many special gifts through the Fund to the 'boys', and he would often visit the Cheery Fund's headquarters, coming up (in his own reported words) 'to be robbed'.

> I shall never forget his first visit to this office [wrote 'Orion', the organiser of the Cheery Fund, in a striking appreciation which revealed the identity of 'Diogenes' two days after his death]. For some time before it we had been fairly regular correspondents owing to the large number of special gifts our old friend sent to the boys. There was usually a jest somewhere in his communications. One day he threatened to give me a 'good beating' with his crutch because of some light reference I had made to 'The Tub' from which he addressed his letters. (I little dreamt then that he owned such a magnificent old place as Bramall Hall.) I laughed back at his crutch threat and promptly forgot all about my letter.
>
> One day Mr Nevill's card was sent up. He came into my room very quickly after it. 'I've come to give you that promised beating with my crutch, you young rascal', he said, walking towards me. I felt as though someone had struck me across the eyes with a whip when I saw under each of his arms a crutch. He stopped my apologies at once.

From that day onwards 'Diogenes' and 'Orion' co-operated in many projects to help forward the Cheery Fund. One incident in particular is mentioned in the newspaper's tribute to Charles Nevill. It concerned a little girl whose father was a marine engineer and who wished to do something to help sailors.

She offered her 'big white pram' to the Cheery Fund [wrote 'Orion']. I didn't want to take it, but I didn't want to hurt her feelings by refusing. 'Diogenes' solved the difficult problem. He bought the 'pram', then asked me to forward a letter to Veronica . . . It was a beautiful letter asking her to accept the 'pram' back from him. It also contained a sovereign to be used as the nucleus of a collection that she hoped to make among her friends. 'You can't encourage that spirit in them too young', 'Di' remarked to me. He was always doing similar things.[30]

Charles Nevill died on 13 September 1916 and was buried in Woodford churchyard, where fifteen years earlier his wife had been laid to rest. The sole beneficiary of his will was his nephew and adopted son, Thomas Nevill Carleton Stiff who, in anticipation of the inheritance and with his father's consent, had, years earlier, legally changed his surname to 'Nevill'. In 1910 T. N. C. Nevill had married Celia Mills of 'White Bank House', Stockport, and the couple started their married life at 'The Hall Cottage' which previously had been the home of the Sidebottom family.

As a member of the Territorials, Tom Nevill became liable for immediate call-up on the outbreak of the First World War. By mid-September 1914 he found himself en route for Egypt, with the rank of Staff Captain in the 42nd (East Lancashire) Division, and the following spring his Division set sail for Gallipoli as part of the ill-fated and costly British expedition to the Dardanelles. Illness caused him to be evacuated from Gallipoli and he was found unfit for further service and discharged. When his uncle died, therefore, Tom Nevill was at home and able to take over the management of Bramall Hall immediately, but in less than five years' time the Nevills had decided to leave. There were tremendous difficulties in the upkeep of so large a place as Bramall Hall in the years of depression immediately following the First World War, and Captain Nevill had no heir to look forward to the inheritance.

By the end of October 1921 notices and advertisements in the national press announced the impending sale of Bramall Hall and invited offers to Curtis & Henson, Estate Agents. The same difficulties of upkeep which confronted Captain Nevill must have daunted other private buyers, for a sale could not be effected. The Nevills moved to London, leaving a caretaker in charge and Bramall Hall still 'For Sale'.

In July 1923, when no buyer for Bramall Hall itself had yet been found, there was a six-day sale of furniture conducted by Capes, Dunn & Co., the same firm who in 1877 had auctioned the Davenport furniture. This time an even bulkier catalogue was issued. It listed for sale (among other valuables) a collection of oriental art, pottery from Persia, Assyria,

Greece and Rome, a panel of seventeenth-century Norwegian tapestry, motor cars (quite a luxury then) and a full-size billiard table by Bennett & Co. In this second great sale were dispersed the many treasures and works of art which Charles Nevill had collected on his travels around the world.

Advertisements appearing in the national newspapers[1] described Bramall Hall as 'the finest half-timbered house in the country', 'in a perfect state of preservation', 'a beautiful and picturesque pile' (with electric light and central heating), but brought no purchaser. They did create a good deal of interest both in this country and in the United States, where the name of Bramall Hall must have been still further popularised by the publication, in 1923, of Kate Douglas Wiggin's autobiography, with its chapter entitled 'An English Country House'. 'The notion that the structure might be resolved into sticks and stones, duly numbered and consigned to Massachusetts is not, in these days of so much misplaced ingenuity, wholly fanciful', the *Manchester Guardian* had suggested in 1921,[2] and during the next few years rumour was persistent in the district that Bramall Hall might be transported to America. There could have been little doubt that the Park would then have been quickly sold for building, for the inter-war period of housing development was now under way. In 1925 it was announced that Bramall Hall was to be auctioned and a sixteen-page catalogue of sale was issued. Should the building this time fail to find a purchaser, 'the Mansion will immediately be lotted for the purpose of demolition, and the various panelled rooms, the large quantity of old oak, original carvings, old leaded lights, staircases, flooring, fire places, mouldings, doors, stone roof etc., will be offered by Auction in lots in October next'.[3]

Meanwhile various attempts were being made to preserve Bramall Hall as an ancient monument, though these were not meeting with much success. Letters and articles appeared in the press bemoaning the fact that no public-spirited body seemed to be willing to take an interest in Bramall Hall. 'R.M.H.', of Old Colwyn, for instance, wrote in 1923:

> The dismantling of such a property and subsequent splitting up of the estate into building plots would be an irremediable mistake and a loss to the whole country. For miles round the hall has been a source of pleasure for many years to thousands of visitors on account of its historic interests. Surely . . . a united endeavour on the part of various public authorities could be made to preserve this charming hall in its sylvan environs as a beauty spot for ever.[4]

A similar letter in 1925 from the secretary of the Society for the Protection of Ancient Buildings brought an offer of £500 if a public subscription list could be opened.[5] At the same time the Cheshire committee of the Ancient Monuments Society sent a recommendation to the Ancient Monuments Board that Bramall Hall should be scheduled for protection. No official action was taken, but on 28 May 1925 there appeared in the press an open letter to Captain Nevill from Lord Peel, the First Commissioner of Works, expressing the concern both of his Department and of the Ancient Monuments Board that the old hall might be destroyed or mutilated. 'It would be nothing short of a calamity if anything of the kind were to happen to this beautiful old mansion', he continued. 'There is, unfortunately, very little left of the kind in the country, and I appeal to you not to lend yourself to anything which might endanger the preservation for future generations of such a splendid specimen of architecture.' 'The best thing, if you must part with it', Lord Peel concluded, 'and if no private person wishes to acquire it to live in, would be for some public body interested in the locality to acquire it in order to use it for some public purpose.'[6]

Even as the letter appeared in the press the Stockport Corporation was making an attempt to acquire Bramall Hall for public use. In May 1925 a special committee of the Town Council was empowered to negotiate with Captain Nevill and, on the basis of reports from the Borough Treasurer concerning the financial aspects of upkeep and from the Borough Surveyor concerning the condition of the building, the committee recommended the Town Council to offer £15,000 for the Hall and grounds. At a special meeting on 28 May 1925 the Town Council unanimously approved the report of its special committee, but added as a rider, 'This Council cannot recommend any increase in the suggested price of £15,000'. Later that evening a meeting took place in Hazel Grove attended by representatives of the Cheshire County Council, the Hazel Grove & Bramhall and the Cheadle & Gatley Urban District Councils, the Ancient Monuments Society and the Society for the Protection of Ancient Buildings, at which representatives of the Stockport Town Council reported on their offer for Bramall Hall. The offer, which was the offer of Stockport alone, was duly made to Captain Nevill, but it was declined as being unacceptable for the whole estate. A letter from the agents suggesting £15,000 for the Hall with 37 acres only (instead of 64 acres) was received by the Town Council on 2 July without discussion. It was obvious that the Corporation would make no further offer, and, in fact, the offer which it had made was withdrawn before the day of auction, now very near at hand.[7]

When the auction did take place on Tuesday 21 July 1925, it was a failure. The estate had been divided into five lots, the largest amount of land going with the building itself. One small lot – an acre and a half of land with some brick buildings fronting on to Bramhall Lane – had been sold privately to the Stockport Gas Committee before the date of auction. The other four lots – the Hall and about 63 acres of land – were first offered together, but the bidding 'stuck' at £13,000, which was £2,000 less than Stockport Corporation had offered for the Hall and 64 acres. Next, the Hall plus 51 acres was offered, but this was withdrawn at £12,500 and no bid at all was made for the Hall plus 37 acres of land. The smaller plots were then offered alone, and they in turn were withdrawn as not having reached the reserve price. The *Manchester Guardian* report the following day stated that about sixty or seventy people attended the sale, although only three or four joined in the bidding. Captain Nevill was among those present.

Before the sale commenced the auctioneer had referred to Captain Nevill's efforts to sell the property during the past five years. Many tempting offers had been received for various parts of the Hall, but these had been consistently refused in the hope that the place might be sold entire as a private dwelling. In default of such a sale now, said the auctioneer, the Hall would be offered in lots piecemeal later in the year.

> Thus, according to the instructions given to the auctioneers [commented the *Manchester City News* on the following Saturday] Bramall Hall will be sold in parts in October next. The purchasers will remove their goods as soon as possible, until there will remain nothing, possibly, of this historical mansion except the bare foundations.

But among those who attended the auction sale – in a watching capacity only – was John H. Davies, one of the wealthiest men in Manchester, and a person who was intensely interested in the fate of Bramall Hall. Less than three weeks after the unsuccessful auction he had negotiated a private sale, and himself purchased the whole estate (less the small portion already sold) for the sum of £15,000.

The news of sale was received with acclamation in both the local and national press. 'Bramall Hall saved. Public spirit of a noted sportsman', said the *Daily Dispatch* of 6 August 1925, reminding its readers that the purchaser was President of Manchester United Football Club and largely responsible for the Old Trafford football ground. 'Saved! Beauty preserved', was the heading of the article in the *Manchester Evening News*, which contained a statement by Mr Davies that he had bought Bramall Hall because 'it is too sacred a building to be broken up'. The *Manchester Guardian* of 7 August explained that, as a member of antiquarian societies, Mr Davies was 'concerned at the number of fine old buildings which have been given over to the housebreaker in recent years' and it was the threat of demolition which had moved him to action; in his own words he bought Bramall Hall 'to save it from the vandals'. The *Manchester Evening Chronicle* reporter, in a personal interview with the purchaser on the same day, suggested that the problem now so effectively solved might recur on his death. ' "We have won the first round", said Mr Davies. "I am satisfied and derive pleasure from knowing that the public are pleased that this beautiful old hall has been saved from the despoiler. I intend to make the Hall my home . . . As to the future, Mrs Davies has to be specially consulted. She knew the interest I have always displayed in Bramhall and has been the ruling spirit in my determination that the fine old structure must not disappear. She has been the inspiration behind my purchase, and she will probably seal its future". "But", he continued, "you can assure the public that neither of us will adopt a dog-in-the-manger policy. When we have entered into occupation we shall take means to ensure that the general interest in Bramall Hall is satisfied. Special attention will be given to the antiquarian side of that interest, and arrangements will be made for visits to the Hall . . . Its ultimate destination will be carefully considered by Mrs Davies and myself, and the feeling which actuated the purchase will play a prominent part in our joint decision." '[8]

That John Henry Davies should have been the surprise purchaser of Bramall Hall is not, when examined, so completely unexpected, for he was an experienced dealer in property and had made much of his money in this way. He had started life as a stockbroker's clerk, but when he married Amy Cattral he needed some more remunerative occupation, for Amy was the niece and ward of Mr Henry Tate, the sugar magnate, later Sir Henry Tate and founder of the Tate Gallery. The marriage was virtually an elopement, for Henry Tate was against the match, considering young Davies to be not good enough for his niece. When Amy had chosen for herself, and was leaving her uncle's house, Davies is reputed to have said, 'I'll never rest, Amy, until I've put you in a house as big as the one you are leaving today'. This vow he fulfilled years later when he took his wife to live in Moseley Hall, Cheadle, then in a house in Knutsford to which he gave the name of Moseley Hall, and finally in Bramall Hall.

After his marriage John Davies went into the estate business, and as he began to make money he bought up rows of houses in Manchester, and there were generally off-licences in the end houses of these rows. Thus he was brought into contact with the brewery trade, and in due course found a place on the board of directors of one after another of the brewery companies. Gradually his became the controlling hand; he arranged amalgamations of companies until finally Walker & Homfrays with its subsidiaries – of every one of which he was the chairman – dominated the brewery trade of Manchester and district.

The perpetual strain and travelling involved in his business deals and the management of his companies was by 1925 already beginning to affect John Davies's health. He had been the owner of Bramall Hall for only two years when he fell seriously ill with heart disease and was told by his doctor that he had not long to live. Not wishing to die at Bramall Hall and leave his wife with a huge estate on her hands and none but sad memories regarding it, he took a furnished house in Llandudno on the pretext of getting a change of air.

The manner of John Davies's passing, as related later by his daughter, Elsie Partington, is strange. The autumn gales, noted for their severity along the North Wales coast, were particularly severe that year, and on the evening of Monday, 24 October 1927, there was a furious storm. In Bramhall, too, there was a terrible storm and the old butler, making his usual telephone call to the Davies family at Llandudno, related how he and other members of the staff thought they heard the sound of horses' hoofs in the courtyard of the Hall. He had gone to open the main door, but found it blown open of itself, and down the drive he heard the sound of horses' hoofs dying away in the distance. He had then locked up, and reported everything now normal. So great was the storm that a stout oak tree in the Park was blown down that night. On that night, too, John Henry Davies died.

It was some years later that Mr Davies's family were introduced to the story of the 'Red Rider', which they read in shortened form on the back of a cigarette card. This legend of Bramall Hall had been given ballad form by John Leigh in the late-nineteenth century. First there is the crashing storm, then the sound of horses' hoofs, the clanging of the portal bell, and the strange rider received into the Hall. In spite of the sinister message which the stranger brings, the knight of Bramhall welcomes his guest and commands that he be given food, drink and shelter.

'And as for thy missives I fear them not!
At peace with my neighbours all ...'

The stranger is given a bed for the night; the following morning the storm is over.

The sun was up when the servitors rose,
And many a scattered bough
Told of the storm on that fearful night,
And many a tree laid low.

But the stranger's horse was nowhere seen,
And the stranger himself had fled;
And stretched on his couch, with peaceful mien,
The good old knight lay dead.[9]

John Davies, too, had known and accepted his fate, and had made provision for leaving this world. He was buried in the Southern Cemetery, Manchester, after a service in Cheadle Parish Church. Before the funeral the coffin, covered with purple and surrounded by flowers, lay in state in the great hall at Bramhall.

In due course Amy Davies returned to Bramall Hall, where the threads of life were picked up again. John Davies had left all his possessions, absolutely, to his wife – in itself an act of great trust in her – and she responded by carrying on life at the Hall as before, just as her husband had desired. Elsie Partington and her family moved to 'The Hall Cottage', which they renamed 'The Dower House', and it was the object of widow and daughter that the Hall should be both a social centre and a centre of historic interest in the neighbourhood. For seven more years this was so. Fêtes and garden parties were frequent occurrences, and many people in the district had opportunity to view the inside of the building.

But such a life could not continue indefinitely and when an opportunity came to repurchase her old home, Moseley Hall, Cheadle, Amy Davies decided to take it. During the ten years which had passed since Bramall Hall had last been for sale there had been a spate of building in Bramhall and the speculative builder had moved in. Bramall Park was immediately seen as a very profitable investment for building development, and some considerable offers were made in order to obtain the land for this purpose. Amy Davies was loyal to her husband's memory and said 'No'. When, however, the Hazel Grove & Bramhall Urban District Council made a move towards purchase, they were met with every encouragement.

This time there were members of the local Council who were determined not to let pass the opportunity to acquire Bramall Hall. At an Extraordinary Meeting held on 26 March 1935 the Council unanimously resolved to purchase the Hall and sixty-two acres of surrounding land on the basis of the District Valuer's valuation of the estate, subject to the approval of the Ministry of Health, and with a contribution by the Cheshire County Council towards the cost. It was also understood, and accepted, that there would be certain conditions of use laid down by the vendor.

The conveyance was signed on 7 October 1935 and at a total cost of £14,360 Bramall Hall passed into public ownership. The Cheshire County Council contributed £3,000 of this amount and the remaining purchase price of £11,000, plus £360 for legal costs, was raised on mortgage by the Hazel Grove & Bramhall Urban District Council. The conditions of use finally agreed between Mrs Davies and the Council concerned both the Hall and the Park. So far as the Park was concerned the Council promised 'for ever hereafter to keep [it] open and unbuilt upon'. In respect of the Hall they bound themselves 'for ever hereafter to keep and maintain in good structural repair and condition the historic mansion house known as Bramall Hall and so that the character thereof shall not be altered by reason of any addition or structural alterations thereto and use the same for the general purposes of the Council (except housing)'.[10]

The Dower House was excluded from the sale and given by Amy Davies to her daughter. In the early part of 1935 Mrs Davies moved back to Moseley Hall, Cheadle, and there she died two years later.

Of all the attributes of John and Amy Davies the two most obvious were their wealth and their generosity. Remembered by the children of his gardener at Knutsford as the man who would put a shilling or a half-crown piece on the window ledge of their cottage when he passed – with the understanding that the first child to find it could keep it – John Davies was remembered by the inhabitants of Bramhall as the person whose public-spirited action saved Bramall Hall from demolition. 'Mr Davies hated to be associated with a failure', said the Rector of Cheadle in a funeral tribute. 'Any man who had that feeling would sooner or later attain the best kind of success'.[11] It was left to John Davies's wife loyally to finish his work and to negotiate a safe settlement for Bramall Hall.

Chapter 9   THE TREASURES OF BRAMALL HALL

On Sunday, 19 April 1936, the day following the official opening ceremony, Bramall Hall was open to view, and the first members of the public were taken round by the newly-appointed caretaker, S. F. Wilson. Sydney Wilson already knew Bramall Hall and grounds well, for he had been in the employ of John H. Davies, first in Knutsford and later in Bramhall, where he was in charge of outside work. His appointment was continued, in a different capacity, by the Hazel Grove & Bramhall Urban District Council and, with his daughter, Shirley, who in June 1936 became his officially-appointed assistant, he took great pride and joy in keeping the building in beautiful condition and making visitors feel welcome and interested.

At the end of that year the Wilson family moved in to the north wing of Bramall Hall, and there they stayed until S. F. Wilson reached retirement in 1951. They saw no ghosts and felt the atmosphere of Bramall Hall to be a happy one. People from all over the country, and, indeed, from all over the world, came to visit this famous Hall, and American visitors, in particular, would come quite long distances out of their way to see it.

From the first the Hazel Grove & Bramhall Urban District Council were intensely proud of their possession of the building, and would use it for important official functions. The proclamation locally of George VI as king in place of his brother, Edward VIII, was read in the grounds of Bramall Hall by Councillor Carrol Allen, Chairman of the Council, in December 1936. With him were the Vice-Chairman (Councillor Reginald Dean), the Clerk, and other members of the Local Authority. As part of the coronation celebrations the following year the front of Bramall Hall was floodlit, and, said the *Stockport Advertiser*, 'seen from many vantage points on the main paths, looks even more lovely than by day'.[1]

During the Second World War the National Fire Service was offered local headquarters in the Hall grounds. The building was kept open for the public, as before, and allied servicemen in uniform were shown round free of charge. In May 1945 came victory in Europe, and a VE Day service of thanksgiving was held on the archery ground on the west of the Hall. A

Victory E gala, with Rose Queen crowning, took place in the grounds in July 1945, and in August, when the end of the war in the far east had been announced, there was a thanksgiving service in the Hall chapel. Again the exterior of the building was floodlit, and this time, besides being beautiful in itself, it symbolised the light which had everywhere returned after years of black-out.

Not until 1946, when the whole country was feeling the economic effects of six years of war, was there a dissentient voice raised in the Urban District Council concerning the desirability of local ownership of Bramall Hall. A motion introduced by four Hazel Grove members on 2 April 1946 suggested the possibility of handing over Bramall Hall to the National Trust. After a heated debate, during which Bramhall members reasserted their pride of possession in Bramall Hall, the motion was defeated.

A very early decision which faced the Hazel Grove & Bramhall Urban District Council after they acquired Bramall Hall concerned the spelling and pronunciation of the name. Old residents called the place 'Brammull', but the spelling 'Bramhall' had become firmly established for the district. During the nineteenth and twentieth centuries the name seemed to have been spelt with or without an 'h' almost according to choice. J. P. Earwaker, the Cheshire antiquarian, had contended that in old deeds in which the place was mentioned the 'h' was almost invariably included and therefore it 'should not be rashly altered now, as it is apt to engender the remark, that if people cannot pronounce it properly, they should, at least, be able to spell it correctly'.[2] Charles Nevill, on the other hand, always used the form 'Bramall' as being closest to that given in the Domesday Book, the earliest authority. 'I look upon Earwaker's remark that "people who are not able to pronounce it, might at any rate spell it rightly", as exceedingly childish', he wrote to his friend, Alfred Burton, 'for those, who like myself, spell and pronounce it Brámall, do so because they consider it the right way, and not from any difficulty in aspirating their hs'.[3] After weighing the evidence, the Council decided to adopt the spelling 'Bramall' for the Hall and Park, while retaining 'Bramhall' for the township, and this distinction has since then been maintained.

During the first years of public ownership there was little furniture in Bramall Hall, for the Urban District Council had no funds which they were allowed to use to purchase furnishings. There were the pieces offered at the time of opening, including the wonderful Paradise Bed which remained in the paradise room for the remainder of Sir William Bromley-Davenport's lifetime, and afterwards until 1957, when it was withdrawn for display at

Capesthorne Hall. There was a bed with rope mattress, specially purchased for Bramall Hall by Charles H. Wrigley, and a large, framed, oil painting, presented by Elsie Partington. This picture, entitled *Widowed, or, Where is my lord the king?* had been specially painted for Charles Nevill by his friend, Herbert Schmalz, and was a Royal Academy exhibit in 1887. Apart from these items the rooms were almost bare. The chapel, however, was in a complete state of disarray. Pews and communion table had disappeared, stained glass had gone from the windows, the floor of the annexe was unmade, and the only furniture consisted of the Davenport pew, a bell cast by William Scott of Wigan in 1665, some loose oak panels stacked round the walls and a nineteenth-century pulpit which had come from Didsbury Parish Church.

The chapel presented a mystery and a challenge. Its history since the Davenports left was virtually unrecorded. Occasional services may have been held in the 1880s but a leaflet which Charles Nevill issued in about 1890 for the benefit of visitors to Bramall Hall contained the information that 'it [the chapel] is at present in a dismantled condition, and will have to undergo very extensive repairs'.[4] The chapel annexe is shown on the ordnance survey map for 1909 and was built by Charles Nevill, probably as an organ chamber. Pipes and part of a console were found in the roof above the chapel room.

To at least one local resident the chapel of 1936 presented a picture of horror, and he could not accept the suggestion that it was to have been restored. He saw it as 'wantonly smashed by some one, otherwise it would not be in its present lamentable state'.[5] It was in the autumn of 1936 (according to his later statements) that Charles Harold Wrigley, head of a Manchester firm of cotton raisers and finishers, who lived in one of the villa residences adjoining the Park, first began seriously to consider the possibility of paying for the restoration of Bramall Hall chapel.

At the same time one of the Urban District Councillors, Reginald Dean, an Independent member since 1930, was feeling the compelling influence of this historic building. He, too, was shocked and saddened by the desecration apparent in the chapel, and when he was elected Chairman of the Council in 1937 he included in his official speech a short appeal. 'Cannot we get the old chapel at Bramall Hall fitted up for occasional use by the Council? [he asked]. A little sojourn there will help us a lot in our work and keep us on the right lines. I shall be a happy man if that can be done.' He slipped this in as just 'a very small matter concerning Bramall Hall on which I want to make an appeal', but it was taken up by the press,[6] and in a very short time Charles Wrigley, Reginald Dean, Joseph Gosling (Chairman of the Parks & Estates Committee) and James Fleming Andrew (the Council's Surveyor) were deeply involved in discussion.

It was agreed at once that the chapel must be refurnished as nearly as possible as it had been in the days of the Davenports, but exact and detailed information seemed impossible to obtain. Had the searchers but known, Alfred Burton's notes could have provided useful information, but Burton's three heavy manuscript volumes were then quite 'undiscovered' so far as their historical content was concerned. They had been stored away, presumably being regarded as interesting mementoes of the Hall in former days rather than as documentary records. Information concerning the lay-out of the chapel was sought first from old residents of the district who had once attended services there. Many were questioned by Charles Wrigley, but none could provide exact information. Help finally came from John Lightfoot, a man who had lived in Bramhall for many years and who, as local correspondent for the *Stockport Advertiser*, had met members of the Davenport family. He wrote to the Rector of Strensham, Rev. A. E. F. C. Davenport, whose daughter, Joan, had attended the official opening of Bramall Hall to the public. The request for information was passed by the Rector to his elder brother, Cyril Davenport, and now came a stroke of good fortune for Bramhall. This brother had in his possession an album of photographs of Bramall Hall taken some time between the years 1855 and 1869.

Correspondence with Cyril Davenport, who was now nearly ninety, was conducted through his married daughter, Mrs Dorothy Davenport-Belt, of St Leonards-on-sea. She sent the album on loan to Bramhall and, to the delight of the searchers, it was found to contain two large photographs showing clearly the lay-out of the chapel, one looking east and one looking west. Charles Wrigley at once instructed his architects, Messrs Oakley & Sanville, to prepare drawings based on the photographs, and to cost the work required to restore the chapel.

By the early part of 1938 it was becoming known in the district that a local resident, who wished to remain anonymous, had undertaken to bear the cost of restoration of Bramall Hall chapel. Charles Wrigley allowed his name to be revealed at the end of March when the plans were finally accepted by the Urban District Council and permission given for the work to be started. At that meeting members of the Council spoke with great enthusiasm of the project to be undertaken. Councillor William Garner, whose father had farmed Lodge Farm as a tenant of the Davenports and who had himself been born on the estate, spoke from his recollections of childhood. 'I was never more delighted as a youngster than when going to the services held at the Hall', he said. Councillor Reginald Dean added that 'those who had seen the plans were amazed at the detail and the magnificence in which the work was to be carried out'.[7]

The following day Charles Wrigley was interviewed by the *Stockport Advertiser*. 'On Wednesday I called to see Mr Wrigley, and found him in the orchard of his lovely garden which overlooks the grounds of Bramall Hall', the reporter wrote. 'He told me that he decided to restore the chapel last October ... As far as possible the old panelling and pews of the chapel will be replaced, and nothing will be done which will be out of keeping with the history of the place ... The old box pews will be made up as far as possible from the ancient woodwork of the chapel which has been recovered. At the east end, on the north side, the old pulpit will be erected [i.e. the pulpit found in the dismantled chapel] and will have stairs leading up to it. New altar rails will have to be provided, as no trace of the old ones has been found. There will be some beautiful oak panelling at the east end. There will be oak panelling under the south and east windows.'[8]

The work continued throughout the summer of 1938. Two box pews, the altar rails and simple bench pews were constructed of solid English oak. Damage to wall and floor was repaired, the aisle relaid and the sanctuary built anew. The roof was cleaned and the woodwork stained. A new east window of nine lights was constructed, and a small window of three lights on the south side. Beneath the windows the walls were panelled with oak. The Urban District Council, as its own contribution, installed the heating and lighting, and rebuilt a portion of the north-east wall.

In May 1938, while dead and decaying wood was being cut from the north wall, a workman discovered an arrow-head lodged in one of the wooden supports. From its position in the centre of the beam it must have been shot into the wood when the oak was still a sapling and remained there for many years until the great trunk of the mature tree was used whole in the building of Bramall Hall chapel. The arrow-head, which must have been between eight hundred and one thousand years old, was put on display in Bramall Hall.

As the work proceeded, gifts were received for the restored chapel. T. N. C. Nevill presented a case of the 1737 prayer books which had been chained to the old pews, Elsie Partington gave two Cromwellian oak tables, one of which was used in place of a communion table, and Charles Wrigley's brother, George Wrigley, gave an American organ. The restoration was complete by autumn except that no pews were placed on the south-west side of the chapel, which was kept for the Davenport box pew.

A large congregation, including representatives of the contractors and many of the workmen as well as councillors, officials and invited guests, filled the newly-erected pews for the re-dedication service on Sunday, 30 October 1938. Local clergy shared the service and, in his address, the Vicar of Bramhall, Rev. John F. Jones, spoke of a wish fulfilled, 'the wish', he said, 'some of us have cherished for many years'.[9]

There is no doubt that in 1938 there was tremendous enthusiasm locally for the restoration of Bramall Hall chapel. There was already talk of regular services to which the public would be invited and a 'chapel sub-committee' soon came into being. A rota was formed of clergy and ministers within the urban district who would be responsible for services at Bramall Hall chapel, each minister being asked to bring an organist and a quartet of singers from his own church to lead the singing. The first such service was held on 15 January 1939, and they have continued on the third Sunday afternoon of the month ever since. For permanent use in Bramall Hall chapel Charles Wrigley provided copies of *Songs of Praise*, and he also had the old bell, found in the derelict chapel, cleaned and rehung in the turret, so that it could be used to summon the congregation to worship.

The first baptism to be held in the restored chapel took place after the monthly service of July 1939, the baby baptised being the granddaughter of Councillor Joseph Gosling. Other baptisms have followed, and the register kept at Bramall Hall records the baptisms of children connected with members and officials of the Council and of children of other residents of the district.

The monthly services maintained their popularity throughout the war years, and it became obvious that pews on the south side, omitted in the reconstruction, were needed in order to complete the seating. Charles Wrigley offered to have the work done as soon as labour and materials again became available. During the winter of 1945–46 four additional bench pews were put in on the south side and a longer bench against the west wall, making the seating agree as nearly as possible with that shown in the old photographs. The Davenport pew was moved to the chapel annexe.

Even so the chapel was not so complete as the enthusiasts would have it. Councillor Leonard Cookson, now Chairman of the Parks & Estates Committee, had discovered that four panels of stained glass which had once formed part of the east and south windows of Bramall Hall chapel had been purchased by the Victoria & Albert Museum in 1927. The glass was mentioned in Earwaker's description of the chapel in 1877. There was 'a representation of the Crucifixion ... much mutilated' in the central light of the east window, and a group of three panels – a Crucifixion, with St John and the Virgin Mary on either side – in the easterly window on the south side.[10] Negotiations were opened with the Museum, and in the summer of 1947 the three panels forming the 'Crucifixion group' were offered on loan. Charles Wrigley paid for their insertion in the lights of the east window of Bramall Hall chapel, and during the monthly service of October 1947 (which was also the Harvest Festival service) the panels were formally re-dedicated to the glory of God.

These three panels are of late-fifteenth- or early-sixteenth-century date, and have been described as 'amongst the best preserved figures from main lights' of window glass in Cheshire.[11] The fourth, mutilated, panel, which was of fourteenth-century date, had been repaired at the Museum by insertion of a fragment from a similar panel of glass. Some years after the restoration on loan to Bramall Hall chapel of the 'Crucifixion group', there was a suggestion to use funds of the society known as the Friends of Bramall Hall in order to procure return of this older, single Crucifixion panel to Bramall Hall. This proved unfeasible, as the panel was still required for display in the Victoria & Albert Museum.

The 'Friends of Bramall Hall' had come into being in 1947 as a direct result of the return to Bramall Hall of another historic treasure – the heraldic tapestry of the Davenports. Reginald Dean, writing for the society some years later, gave his own account of this acquisition, of which he was the instigator and prime inspiration.

> Following the acquisition of Bramall Hall by the Hazel Grove & Bramhall Urban District Council in 1935, there was a natural desire to obtain furnishings for the Hall. The Council was fortunate in the receipt of a number of valuable gifts, entirely in keeping with the Hall, and also in the reconstruction of the Chapel by the late Mr Charles H. Wrigley. It was, however, still felt that complete satisfaction could be achieved only by the return to the Hall of some of the old Davenport furnishings. Fortunately, there were available a number of newspaper cuttings in which were listed each day the more important items sold at Bramall Hall on the preceding day. As usual in such records, however, the information was limited to the amount realised and the surname of the purchaser. Generally that information was of little, if any, help. But in regard to the most important of all the items in the Plaster Room it

appeared that the purchaser was a Mr Christy, he having bought the Heraldic Tapestry for the sum of £25.

With the assistance of Colonel Christie-Miller [i.e. the late Sir Geoffry Christie-Miller] of Stockport, it was ascertained that the Heraldic Tapestry was in the ownership of Mr H. A. Christy, then resident near Builth Wells, in the heart of Wales. Correspondence with Mr H. A. Christy [son of Stephen Christy] resulted in his agreement to send the Tapestry to Bramall for inspection, with a view to its ultimate acquirement for the Hall at a price of £250, the sum for which it had been insured.

The Urban District Council not having funds for the purchase of furnishings for the Hall, it was necessary to endeavour to raise the money privately and a number of prominent local residents were invited to a Meeting at the Hall with a view to enlisting their interest and assistance in this matter. There was a most welcome response, and the Meeting, held on 14th May 1945, was well attended. The Tapestry was suspended on the end wall of the Great Hall, where it could easily be seen and appreciated, and its story and some explanation of its design and meaning were given to the Meeting. There was then a short adjournment for a cup of tea, affording the opportunity for individual examination of the Tapestry, and also for some unofficial canvassing of those present. But such canvassing proved unnecessary, for, during the tea interval, Mr W. Neild Dixon, of Bramhall, very generously undertook himself to bear the whole cost of purchase of the Tapestry, and then to present it to the Hall for reinstatement in its old position in the Plaster Room.[12]

At the 'Tapestry meeting' described above the interest was so great that there was talk of forming a permanent association to help with the acquisition of suitable furnishings for Bramall Hall. Several subscriptions towards the purchase price of the tapestry had already been received, and an ad hoc committee was empowered to use the money for repairing and cleaning the tapestry and mounting it in a large frame. At a similar meeting just one year later the tapestry was formally handed over by its purchaser, W. Neild Dixon, and accepted on behalf of the Urban District Council by Councillor Dean, then just entering on his second term as Chairman of the Council. An originating committee for a 'Hall association' was then appointed under the new chairman.

The public inaugural meeting of the 'Friends of Bramall Hall' (as the organisation came to be called) was held on Wednesday, 24 July 1946 under the chairmanship of Mrs Lilian Bromley-Davenport (deputising for Sir William), and about 140 people attended. The objects of the society, as defined by the originating committee and accepted by the meeting, were:

> The promotion of interest in Bramall Hall
> Advice and assistance in respect of the furnishings of the Hall
> Advice and assistance in the maintenance and improvement of the Hall
> and its grounds.

A programme of meetings had already been arranged for the first session, and paid-up members would be allowed admission to Bramall Hall free of charge during normal hours of opening and subject to the usual restrictions imposed by the Urban District Council. Councillor Leonard Cookson, who had been one of the first to bring up the idea of such a society, appealed for public support.

At the first annual general meeting in May 1947 the constitution of the Friends of Bramall Hall, which had already been approved by the Urban District Council, was formally adopted. It was realised that close liaison must be maintained with the Council (the ultimate authority on all matters concerning the Hall) and some councillors would serve ex-officio on the committee of the 'Friends'. Already there had been co-operation between representatives of the 'Friends' and the Council when, in the summer of 1946, they met Mrs Dorothy Davenport-Belt, daughter of Cyril Davenport, on her visit to the Hall. At the annual general meeting in 1947 the society was able to present to the Council an album containing professional reproductions of all Mrs Belt's interesting interior photographs, for permanent display in Bramall Hall. Now began a period of special effort to trace, and perhaps to purchase from the funds of the society, items which had a special significance for Bramall Hall. For eighteen years, until he left Bramhall in 1964, Reginald Dean held the position of chairman of the committee of the Friends of Bramall Hall. Mrs Gladys Lawton, who in 1948 became its honorary secretary, served for an even longer period, and together these two were responsible for much of the behind-the-scenes work which resulted in many interesting acquisitions for Bramall Hall.

Gradually more and more reminders of its past history found their way back to the Hall, sometimes offered to the Urban District Council direct, sometimes through the Friends of Bramall Hall acting as intermediaries. Here are details of some of the major additions from 1946.

> 1946 Mrs Dorothy Davenport-Belt presented a portrait in oils of her great-grandfather, Salusbury Pryce Humphreys (as he then was), for display in the library. Later that year she donated a

woollen rug, made by her father, Cyril Davenport, and worked with the arms of Queen Elizabeth I as depicted on the overmantel in the withdrawing room.

1949 Katharine Sidebottom offered back to Bramall Hall the slab of marble which, so she had understood from her mother, had once served as a communion table in the chapel. It had been incorporated in a kitchen table, used by the Sidebottom family when they lived at The Hall Cottage. The restorers of Bramall Hall chapel had assumed that the communion table (shown on the old photograph as railed in) was made of wood, as was customary in post-Reformation times. However, Alfred Burton had described the communion table as 'a small slab of fossil marble fixed to the wall under the east window', and his description confirmed a statement which appeared in the *Manchester Courier* at the time of the great sale, 'The altar is of polished mountain limestone, fitted with fossils'.[13] Before the marble-topped table was accepted, it was carefully inspected by Messrs Dean, Cookson, Andrew and Wrigley. The marble was found to be unpolished along one side, and this was consistent with its being fitted to the wall. It was agreed that the table should be displayed in the Nevill chapel annexe.

1949 Charles Wrigley paid for the cleaning, repolishing and lacquering of the fine candelabra in the withdrawing room. Later this year he returned, for use in the chapel, the inscribed Bible which had been presented to him by the Urban District Council in 1939. The Bible contained on its fly-leaf the signatures of all members of the Council serving at the time of the chapel restoration. Before it was formally returned further fly-leaves were inserted, providing place for Charles Wrigley's own signature and request that the Bible should be used in the chapel 'in perpetuity', and the signed acceptance of the Chairman of the Council of 1949 and his colleagues.

1950 Twenty-four of the Davenport ancestral portraits, a plaster model of the felon's head crest and two oak door capitals which had once stood above the north and south doors in the withdrawing room were received back on permanent loan from D. J. Davenport-Handley Esq., of Clipsham.

1951 A portrait in oils of Captain T. N. C. Nevill, showing him as a young man in full military uniform, was presented by his widow, Celia Nevill.

1952–53 The Friends of Bramall Hall paid for a much-needed repair and restoration to the library, making it a suitable room for display of some of the smaller items of furniture and trinkets which were now being acquired.

1957 Mrs Davenport-Belt died. Her bequest to Bramall Hall included an old Bible box containing various lecture notes of her father, Cyril Davenport (who had been a librarian in the British Museum), the scrapbook of her mother, Georgina Davenport, and the old album of photographs of Bramall Hall. Thus the photographs of the 1860s, from which so much had been learned, found their permanent home in Bramall Hall.

1957 The Friends of Bramall Hall paid for the expert cleaning of three of the Davenport ancestral portraits on loan to the Hall.

1958 The Friends of Bramall Hall commissioned a water-colour reproduction of a small portion of the Davenport heraldic tapestry. The tapestry had been worked in wool on a blue ground, but much of the blue material had disappeared, leaving only the strong linen foundation as a background. The copy was displayed beneath the tapestry in order to give visitors some idea of the original brilliance of the colours.

1958 D. J. Davenport-Handley added to his permanent loan to Bramall Hall a very fine pedigree roll of the Davenport family of Bramhall. The Friends of Bramall Hall provided a glass exhibition case for its display in the withdrawing room.

1959 The Friends of Bramall Hall paid for the cleaning of three further Davenport portraits, and for the making of full-size photographs of the portraits of Sir William and Dame Dorothy Davenport, which were still at Clipsham Hall. These photographs were framed and hung in the great hall at Bramall Hall.

1961 Various items of former 'Nevill' furniture, which were offered for sale in Alderley Edge, were identified and repurchased for Bramall Hall by the 'Friends'. In particular, an oak Cromwellian table, with modern top, found an appropriate place in the centre of the great hall.

1963 Various Davenport relics, including an old box trunk used by Sir Salusbury when he was a young officer at sea and a spinning wheel made for Lady Davenport were purchased by the Friends of Bramall Hall from a descendant of Lady Davenport's personal maid.

1963 D. J. Davenport-Handley added three more oil paintings to his loan of ancestral portraits already made to Bramall Hall, together with a leather-bound Bible and a Prayer Book which had been presented to Bramall Hall chapel by the Rector of St Thomas's, Stockport, in 1851, and a replica of Bramall Hall given to John William Handley Davenport as a wedding present in 1876.[14]

1970 The mural paintings in the ball room were professionally restored under the direction of the Department of the Environment, the cost being met by grants from various sources and a donation from the Friends of Bramall Hall. The work involved first the removal, particularly on the north wall, of discolouring shellac (Charles Nevill's carriage varnish?) and then repeated spraying with lime water to consolidate the plaster support and fix and strengthen the colour. A limited amount of retouching was carried out with dry colour skimmed milk and lime water, but no attempt made to reconstruct any of the design where this had become lost or damaged. The mural decorations, long recognised to be one of the chief treasures of the building, now became also one of the greatest attractions of Bramall Hall for the visitor.

1972 The painting *Rabboni* by Herbert Schmalz was given to Bramall Hall by the Vicar and churchwardens of St Luke with St Paul, Brinnington, Stockport, when the church of St Paul, Portwood, was demolished. The picture is the last of a series of three dealing with the closing events of Christ's life, which were inspired by Schmalz's visit to the Holy Land in 1890, and it shows the profound religious feeling of the artist. It had been given to St Paul's church by Captain Nevill.

Generous support for the Friends of Bramall Hall had come immediately on its formation from the known representatives of families which had connections with Bramall Hall, but in the early days there was no contact with any member of the family of John William Handley Davenport; indeed, no-one on the committee of 1947 knew whether there was a descendant of the last Davenport of Bramhall still living. That knowledge came fortuitously, through an article in the *Manchester Guardian*.

During the air-raids on London in 1940 the House of Commons had suffered extensive damage, and rebuilding became a priority when the War was over. The work was within six months of completion when, on Monday, 26 September 1949, the *Manchester Guardian* carried an article, with two photographs, describing the stone, 'the best from the weathering of a thousand years', which was being used for the new building. The article was entitled 'The centuries-old quarries of Clipsham' and it included a reference to 'Mr D. J. Davenport-Handley, the young squire of Clipsham, who owns and directs the quarries in succession to his father and grandfather'.

The name, with its implications, was carefully noted by Reginald Dean, who unfailingly read his morning newspaper from beginning to end. On 4 October 1949 he wrote to the squire of Clipsham on Friends of Bramall Hall official notepaper.

Unless I am much mistaken [he wrote] your grandfather was that Mr J. W. Handley Davenport who, having succeeded to the Bramall Estate in 1869 (on the death of his father) sold that Estate in 1877, thus terminating the centuries-long connection of the Davenport family with Bramhall. It was following this sale that the development of modern Bramhall began.

If I am correct, you will, I am sure, be interested to know that, following further private ownership, Bramall Hall and Park were, in 1935, acquired by the Hazel Grove & Bramhall Urban District Council, and such are now maintained by the Council for the benefit of the general public. The Hall is in excellent condition, and is of great interest to the many thousands of visitors who come to view it, from far and near.

Unfortunately, the Hall is rather bare of furniture, and a society of 'Friends of Bramall Hall' has been formed with the object of assisting the Local Council, particularly in regard to furnishings. I enclose a Brochure of the society, which I think you will find of interest.

We are also most anxious to obtain information relative to the past history of the Hall, and of the old Davenport family. Much has already been learned, but, if you can assist further we should indeed be grateful.

A reply from Mr Davenport-Handley (he had now discontinued the use of his third surname of 'Humphreys') was dated 1 November 1949.

You are correct in assuming that my Grandfather sold Bramall in 1877 and came to Clipsham. I regret to say however that I have never seen Bramall.

Although we have several pictures and a model of it here, I am afraid we have no details regarding its history.

Should you ever be in this district I should be very pleased to show you some of the ancestral pictures, which doubtless came from Bramall, and if you are interested I could, perhaps, let you have some of them for your society to replace in their old surroundings.

This simple statement concerning the whereabouts of the ancestral portraits came as a complete surprise, the only known fact then being that they had been removed by J. W. H. Davenport prior to the 1877 sale. In January 1950 Reginald Dean visited Clipsham, after having been given full authority by the Hazel Grove & Bramhall Urban District Council to accept for Bramall Hall such portraits as might be offered.

Some of the more important Davenport portraits he saw displayed on the walls at Clipsham Hall. Here were the portraits of Sir William and Dame Dorothy Davenport, the bridal picture of their eldest son's child wife, Frances Wilbraham, and the joint portrait of that same son (the sixth William Davenport) with his second wife, Margaret. Other portraits were stored away, unlabelled and unidentifiable by the present members of the Davenport-Handley family. With the help of descriptions given in Earwaker's *East Cheshire* and the interior photographs of Bramall Hall copied from the Davenport-Belt album, Reginald Dean was able to trace many of the portraits as having once hung on the walls of Bramall Hall, and in some cases he could identify their subjects exactly. He was able to select over twenty of the stored portraits for loan to Bramall Hall, but even more to him than the actual loan was the happily-renewed link between Bramhall and its own branch of the Davenport family.

The portraits arrived at Bramall Hall the following month and Reginald Dean spent much time with the Surveyor, James Fleming Andrew, examining, listing and labelling them. Those which could be identified included the portraits of John and Margaret Warren (parents of Dame Dorothy Davenport), the seventh William Davenport, his wife (Elizabeth), four of their young children, his sister (Mrs Margaret Clayton) and his brother-in-law (Robert Tatton), the tenth William Davenport and his wife (Martha) and, finally, Mrs Diana Elizabeth Davenport. The portrait of the Lady Abbess, painted in 1616 in the 49th year of her age, and noted but not identified by Earwaker, remained – and still remains – an enigma. It could only be assumed that she was of Davenport descent, but she must at that date have belonged to a continental order, for all English orders had been suppressed.

The Hazel Grove & Bramhall Urban District Council had invited David Davenport-Handley, with his wife, Leslie, to visit Bramhall on

Saturday, 20 May 1950, for the formal handing-over of the pictures to Bramall Hall. Many members of the Friends of Bramall Hall, as well as members and officials of the Council, were present when the Squire of Clipsham presented the picture of Diana Elizabeth Davenport, his great-grandmother, as a token portrait to the Chairman of the Council, Councillor Frank Swindell.

For the 1950 Christmas meeting of the 'Friends', Councillor Dean's wife wrote short scenes based on the principal characters in the Davenport portraits, conveying in dramatic form the few known facts of their lives and relationships. The scenes were depicted by members of the society in the lower banqueting room at Bramall Hall. There, in imagination, ghosts of the Davenports of Bramhall, from the seventeenth to the nineteenth centuries, stepped from their frames, greeted one another over the years, and returned happy because they were home at last. [15]

Chapter 10   THE HALL AS HISTORY

Those men who in 1935 undertook the maintenance of Bramall Hall on behalf of the public possessed, at first, little detailed knowledge of its history. On the day of the official opening they relied on two well-known Stockport antiquaries – Harry Ashton Potter and Herbert Morton – to conduct visitors round the building and explain its history. Within a few years, however, an expert on the history of Bramall Hall had arisen from among the Hazel Grove & Bramhall Urban District Council's own members.

By late 1937 Reginald Dean had become deeply involved in the plans for restoration of Bramall Hall chapel, and the search for accurate information about the chapel stimulated his interest in many other aspects of the Hall's history. After he had been elected Chairman of the Parks & Estates Committee in April 1941 he commenced an intensive study of the Burton Manuscripts, which occupied his spare time for many months. This was for him a matter of interest and a method of improving his knowledge of the building which it was the duty of his committee to administer; it became, for the district, a rediscovery of the work of a local antiquarian, with a new realisation of its value.

On Wednesday, 11 March 1942 – in the midst of the War years – Reginald Dean was invited to speak to the boys of the Hazel Grove Council School (as it then was) on the subject of Bramall Hall. This proved to be the first of a long series of lectures freely given by him in Bramhall, Hazel Grove, Woodford and nearby districts over the next twenty and more years. The first major occasion was a 'Lantern Lecture on Bramall Hall and its history' organised officially by the Hazel Grove & Bramhall Urban District Council and held in the Hazel Grove Wesley School on Thursday, 18 March 1943. Small advertisement leaflets said 'Bramall Hall is owned by the Ratepayers. Take this opportunity to hear about it.' About three hundred people attended, and a further two hundred heard the lecture in Bramhall that same spring, either at local church meetings or in connection with the local 'Wings for Victory Campaign'.

Some of the $3\frac{1}{4}$in. x $3\frac{1}{4}$in. glass slides used on these early occasions were specially made from negatives provided by Charles Smith who, as local reporter for the *Stockport Advertiser*, was particularly interested in the history of Bramhall. They formed the nucleus of a collection on historic Bramhall which grew with the years; Arthur Holland, William Kemp and Cephas Rhodes, to name but a few old residents, were generous in supplying pictures and information. Perhaps the most valuable gift in the very early days was a choice collection of glass slides which had once belonged to Reginald Dean's close neighbour, John Pettigrew. These pictures of Bramall Hall and the buildings in and around the village of Bramhall were taken in the first quarter of the twentieth century.

In September 1944 Reginald Dean acquired another interesting collection of glass slides which provided the inspiration for a new lecture illustrating the growth of the village of Bramhall after the sale of the Bramall Hall estate. It was first given at a meeting of the Brookdale Social Club on 8 March 1945.

> So many people were unable to gain admittance to the assembly hall of the Ladybrook Hotel on Thursday evening last for the lantern lecture on 'Bramhall, past and present' by Councillor Reginald Dean, that he has been requested to repeat the lecture at an early date. [reported the *Stockport Advertiser* on 16 March]
>
> The lecture forms an admirable pendant to Councillor Dean's lecture on Bramall Hall, which he has already given a dozen times in the district. This was the first time he had dealt with the general history of Bramhall and his remarks were illustrated by a fine collection of lantern slides, made by the late Mr William Galloway . . . They show Bramhall as it was fifty years ago.

In 1946 Reginald Dean was introduced to the Diary of Charles Bellairs by Mrs (later Dame Lilian) Bromley-Davenport, and he at once saw the possibilities of a new and interesting talk on the Davenport family combined with a reading of the Diary. 'Davenport of Bramall and Isherwood of Marple' was first given to the Friends of Bramall Hall at their March 1947 meeting. After a brief description of the Davenport and Isherwood families in 1838 (the year of the Diary), there followed a reading of the Diary and slides showing the exterior of Marple Hall (then still standing), the route the visitors would take as they made their way down Bridge Lane and along the drive to Bramall Hall, and the interior of Bramall Hall in Davenport days.

For the third annual general meeting of the Friends of Bramall Hall in May 1949 a talk entitled 'The Home at the Hall', dealing with life in Nevill days, was given. For this Reginald Dean received help from Katharine Sidebottom, the niece of Charles and Mary Nevill, and new slides were made from some of her photographs.

As the War years receded and life returned to normal requests for lectures became more frequent, and Reginald Dean visited youth organisations, townswomen's guilds, church fellowships, Mothers' Union branches, literary and historical societies and, in fact, any organisations which expressed an interest in his subject and were able to provide an audience. The record of the Lancashire & Cheshire Antiquarian Society, made after their visit to Bramall Hall in July 1955, can speak for all:

> Leader, Councillor Reginald Dean, F.C.A., an authority on the hall and Davenport family, who gave an entertaining and instructive talk and conducted the party round the hall, one of the finest remaining examples of a half-timbered Tudor manor house (1590/1600) with a south wing probably dating back to 1400.[1]

Like Alfred Burton (who was also an accountant) Reginald Dean would have liked to incorporate his findings in book form. Burton had obviously hoped to publish a history of Bramall Hall up to the late-nineteenth century, and in 1887 he stated that this was 'only awaiting the outcome of the present repairs'.[2] He died on 25 November 1890, the work unfinished. Eighty years later there was still no printed history of Bramall Hall. Failing health had prevented Reginald Dean from undertaking the work, and he died in Lincoln on 12 March 1970.

As its contribution to European Architectural Heritage Year 1975, the Victoria & Albert Museum mounted an exhibition, *The Destruction of the English Country House 1875-1975*. It showed vividly the appalling devastation which, during a hundred years, had been taking place among country houses, England's most typical and beautiful contribution to the world's architecture. Miraculously Bramall Hall escaped. It no longer forms part of the green county of Cheshire; Davenports, Nevills and Davieses have gone, and the Hazel Grove & Bramhall Urban District Council has ceased to exist, merged with other local authorities in 1974 to form the Stockport Metropolitan Borough Council within the Greater Manchester conurbation. But Bramall Hall still stands in its once broomy nook, a silent tribute to the men and women who, over many years, have recognised the truth of the words

This house is one of the treasures of England.

E'en like some wrinkled grand-maternal face,
Among Time's changes and decays still spared,
Whose furrowed features bear the ploughshare trace
Of all the loads of sorrow she has shared:
So, ancient Bramhall, in thy rustic chair
Thou sit'st, and on the passing world look'st down
Impassively serene, nor smile, nor frown,
Disturbs the tenour of thy tranquil air.

What smiling morns have glistened in those eyes,
What silent evenings crept from out yon glen!
What pangs and fears, what loves and hates of men
Have rived thy heart these brooding centuries!
May health and wealth long o'er thy threshold roam
And keep thee what thou art — an English Home.

NOTES

Introduction

1 See *Stockport Express*, 23 April 1936, and, *Stockport Advertiser*, 24 April 1936 (from which quotations are taken).

Chapter 1   The glory of Bramall Hall

1 *Old Halls in Lancashire and Cheshire*, p. 147.
2 *Early Renaissance Architecture in England*, 2nd edn. (1914), pp. 118–19.
3 Chapter 4.
4 For a description see: F. Sydney Eden, 'Heraldic glass at Bramall Hall', in *The Connoisseur* (Oct. 1931), pp. 253–6.
5 Antiquus (pseud.), 'Bramhall and the Davenports', in *North Cheshire Herald*, 6 April 1882.
6 John Leigh, 'The Maid of Bramhall Hall', in *Lays and Legends of Cheshire* (c. 1880), p. 48.
7 See Winifred J. Haward, *The Secret Rooms of Yorkshire* (1956), pp. 60–61.
8 p. 449.

Chapter 2   Domesday Bramhall and the Bromales

1 *The Manor*, p. 763.
2 F. Moorhouse, 'On the earthwork in Crow Holt Wood, near Bramhall Hall, Cheshire', in *Trans. Lancs. & Ches. Antiquarian Society*, vol. 27 (1909), p. 82.
3 J. Tait, ed., *The Domesday Survey of Cheshire* (1916), p. 181.
4 Quoted by Earwaker, p. 423.

Chapter 3 Davenport of Bramhall – 400 years of male succession

1 For various versions see: T. W. Barlow, ed., *The Lancs. & Ches. Historical Collector*, vol. 1 (1853), pp. 26–7; vol. 2 (1855), pp. 55–6; *Cheshire Notes & Queries*, vol. 1 (1882), pp. 183–4; Jesse Lee, *Heraldica Lancastria* (Manchester Reference Library MS), vol. 2, opp. D115.

2 *Materials for a History of the Reign of Henry VII*, ed. by W. Campbell (Rolls series, no. 60 1873–77), vol. 2, p. 30. William Davenport's annuity was one of sixteen such grants made on the same day, 3 September 1486.

3 *37th Report of the Deputy Keeper of the Public Records* (1876), appendix 2, p. 352.

4 ed. Lucy Toulmin Smith (1906–10), vol. 5, p. 27.

5 *Lancs. & Ches. Wills and Inventories*, ed. by G. J. Piccope (Chetham Society, vol. 33, 1855), pp. 76–81, from which quotations are taken.

6 W. A. Shaw, *The Knights of England* (1906), vol. 2, p. 55.

7 See *Lancashire Inquisitions: Stuart period*, ed. by J. P. Rylands (Record Society for Lancs. & Ches., vol. 3, 1879), pp. 75–6.

8 Verses publ. by J. P. Earwaker in his chapter on Cheadle Bulkeley township, *East Cheshire*, vol. 1 (1877), p. 176.

9 Quoted by K. R. Wark, *Elizabethan Recusancy in Cheshire* (Chetham Society, 3rd series, vol. 19, 1971), p. 49.

10 Earwaker, p. 438.

11 Shaw, op.cit., p. 102. There is some confusion as to whether the knighting of William Davenport took place before the King left Worksop on the morning of 21 April 1603 or at Newark Castle the following day. The name is found in the lists of knights given for both dates in J. Nichols, *The Progresses of King James I* (1828), vol. 1, pp. 88, 90, but Shaw prefers the later date.

12 See H. W. Clemesha, ed., 'The new court book of the manor of Bramhall 1632–1657', in *Remains Historical and Literary . . . of Lancs. & Ches.* (Chetham Society, new series, vol. 80, 1921), part 3.

13 Earwaker, pp. 429–33, from which all quotations are taken.

14 *The Manor*, p. 820.

15 For history of the school see: Earwaker, p. 455; G. Ormerod (rev. T. Helsby), *History of the County Palatine . . . of Chester* (1882), vol. 3, p. 829; *The Township*, p. 323.

16 *The Manor*, pp. 866–7.

17   Earwaker, p. 434,n. The Society of Friends, Cheshire Monthly Meeting, copy Register of Births (Cheshire Record Office EFC/1/14/1) gives the date of birth of 'Ahsah Starrs' daughter of Caleb and Elizabeth, as 22 June 1711.
18   Earwaker, p. 448. The portraits are unsigned.
19   ibid., p. 441, quoting from Rev. John Watson's *Survey of Bramhall*.
20   G. Ormerod, *History of the County Palatine . . . of Chester* (1819), vol. 3, p. 402.
21   *The Torrington Diaries*, ed. by C. B. Andrews (1934–38), vol. 2, pp. 202–4, from which quotations are taken.
22   This is the view of Mr W. J. Smith of the Lancs. & Ches. Antiquarian Society, who notes Byng's special comment at Stockport and Bramall Hall on this type of decoration.
23   *The Manor*, p. 496.
24   *Palmer MS D*, in Chetham's Library, Manchester.
25   *Stockport Advertiser*, 24 April 1829.

Chapter 4   Davenport of Bramhall – the break in the line

1   Biographical details and accounts of his naval career will be found in John Marshall, *Royal Naval Biography* (1823–25), vol. 2, part 2, pp. 891–7; H. Heginbotham, *Stockport: ancient and modern* (1882–92), vol. 2, pp. 357–9; *Morning Herald*, 20 November 1845.
2   Doe v. Humphreys, knt. The case was factually reported in *Stockport Advertiser*, 21 August 1835, and *Manchester Guardian*, 22 August 1835. A more dramatic description appeared in *Chester Chronicle*, 21 August 1835, from which quotation is taken. See also *A brief account of the Davenports of East Cheshire and a branch therefrom* (printed for private circulation by Reginald Davenport, 1899), ch. 4.
3   Supplement to *Stockport Advertiser*, 21 November 1845.
4   Extracts are taken from typed copy made by Reginald Dean 'from Manuscript loaned to him by Mrs Lilian Bromley-Davenport, of Capesthorne, May 1946'. The derivation of this manuscript is given in a final note:
>   re-copied from a copy made by Jack
>   Bradshaw-Isherwood from a copy made
>   by Eleanor Bellairs from the diary of
>   her Father the Revd Charles Bellairs.

It is not now known whether the original manuscript is still in existence. For further extracts from the Bellairs Diary as it concerns the Isherwood family of Marple, rather than the Davenport family of Bramhall, see Christopher Isherwood, *Kathleen and Frank* (1971).

5   Ormerod (rev. Helsby 1882), vol. 3, p. 826,n. (signed 'H').

6   *Plan of land laid out for building upon the Bramall Hall estate . . . belonging to Lady Davenport* (no date, probably c. 1845–50). Inserted at the front of Burton's MS *The Manor.*

7   16 November 1855. See also 20 & 27 October, 17 November 1854.

8   H. Worthington Barlow, *Cheshire: its historical and literary associations . . .* (1855), pp. 116–17.

9   See 6 above.

10   Dean papers, 29 August 1949.

11   5 March 1869.

12   7 May 1857, with codicil 5 December 1868.

13   9 July 1869, copy in *Abstract of Title of J. W. H. Davenport.*

14   The owners and restorers of Wallbank in 1970 (Mr and Mrs B. G. Mann) discovered the stone in the rubble of the barn, which had been demolished before they took possession.

Chapter 5   Interlude

1   Among the names of principal guests is that of 'W. J. Davenport, Esq.', but I have been enable to identify any Davenport with these initials. J. W. H. Davenport would seem to qualify for such a position, but there is no direct evidence that he was present.

2   *Stockport & Cheshire County News*, 6 September 1872. Extracts from Mr Tipping's speech are also taken from the *County News* report.

3   ibid.

4   *Stockport Advertiser*, 6 September 1872.

5   The change of name was made by Wakefield Christy in 1890 when he succeeded to the estates of his uncle, Samuel Christie-Miller, in Scotland. The spelling 'Christy' is the English and Irish form of the name; 'Christie' is the Scottish.

Chapter 6   John William Handley Davenport and the sale

1   *Manchester Weekly Times*, 5 May 1877;
     Cheshire County News and Stockport Chronicle, 4 May 1877.

2 *Manchester City News*, 12 May 1877;
   The Athenæum, 12 May 1877.
3 8, 9, 10 & 11 May 1877. Descriptions are from the catalogue of sale.
4 *The Manor*, p. 949.
5 *Manchester Courier*, 2 May 1877; *The Athenæum*, 12 May 1877.
6 12 May 1877.
7 *Cheshire County News*, 11 May 1877.
8 *Barritt MS* A.4.72, Chetham's Library, Manchester. The section
   descriptive of Bramhall commences, 'Taking a walk with my friend
   Samuel Hough in the summer of 1777 to Bramall Hall . . .'
9 5 May 1877.
10 *Barritt MS* above.
11 *Manchester City News*, 12 May 1877.
12 *The Manor*, pp. 535–6. Burton gave as reference for his first quotation
   The Times, 9 October 1884, p. 9, c. 4. The remark of Lord Chief
   Justice Crew is there used as an illustration of the working of British
   peerage law, which kept alive the right to a title (even though for long it
   might seem to be in abeyance) until a specific person could legally
   establish proof of succession. Burton gave no reference for his second
   quotation, and I have been unable to trace the statement attributed to
   Dr Johnson.
13 ibid. p. 535.
14 ibid. pp. 902–3, from which details and quotations are taken.
15 31 July 1914. Nearly sixty years later a former Clipsham employee,
   then living in an Old People's Home, near Lincoln, confirmed the truth
   of this statement. Charles Blow remembered 'the old squire' as
   essentially good-hearted, and not without a sense of humour, though he
   was also reserved. Mr Blow recalled how his wife would have her
   weekly washing hanging out before seven o'clock on a Monday
   morning, and the squire, on his round of the estate, would lean over the
   wall and call out, 'You're first, Mrs Blow'. Charles Blow also stated
   that he, with another of the Clipsham workmen, dug the old squire's
   grave and built the vault over it with slabs of stone from the Clipsham
   quarries.

Chapter 7   Bramall Hall – the home of Charles Nevill

1 e.g. *Manchester Guardian*, 19 September 1877; 15 April 1879.

2   'An Intercepted Letter by an Angler's Wife', in *Anglers' Evenings* (Manchester Anglers' Association, 1880), pp. 172–3. The letter, though written by Mary Nevill, was published anonymously.

3   'A Letter from Norway by an Angler's Wife', in *Anglers' Evenings* 2nd series (Manchester Anglers' Association, 1882), pp. 175–6. Like the previous letter, this was published anonymously.

4   C. H. Nevill to Francis Sidebottom, 7 July 1896.

5   *The Manor*, pp. 795, 797.

6   *Domestic Architecture*, p. 618. The south staircase is described in *The Manor*, p. 801, but Burton's photographs ·vould appear to be of the north, or principal, staircase.

7   *The Manor*, p. 816.

8   ibid., pp. 861–2, 863.

9   ibid., pp. 826–7, 825.

10   ibid., pp. 837, 797.

11   ibid., pp. 831–2; *Domestic Architecture*, pp. 630–31.

12   *The Manor*, pp. 814–15. The chapel is described on pp. 803 et seq.

13   ibid., p. 877 for Burton's comments on 'The Maid of Bramhall Hall'; p. 884 for 'The Red Rider'; p. 889 for the Murder legend and for Burton's own remarks concerning ghosts.

14   Chas H. Nevill to Cyril J. Davenport, 17 July 1888. Copy made by R. Dean with note, 'Original letter included with other papers in Bible Box bequeathed to The Urban District Council by Mrs Dorothy (Davenport) Belt in 1957'.

15   *The Manor*, p. 818; Ormerod (1819), vol. 3, p. 402.

16   *The Manor*, pp. 913–15.

17   See 14 above.

18   ibid.

19   *Trans. Lancs. & Ches. Antiquarian Society*, vol. 5 (1887), p. 302.

20   *The Manor*, pp. 776, 777–8.

21   ibid., pp. 898–9.

22   ibid., pp. 892–3. The poem, of which verses 7 and 9 are quoted, is dated 16 August 1888. No other source is given.

23   K. D. Wiggin, *My Garden of Memory* (1923). This quotation and the extracts from two letters following form part of chapter 20, 'An English Country House', which deals almost entirely with Bramall Hall.

24   N. A. Smith, *Kate Douglas Wiggin as her sister knew her* (1925), p. 333.

25   See *Cheshire Daily Echo*, 4 July 1896.

26 Dean papers, 20 December 1947.
27 C. H. Nevill to Francis Sidebottom, 7 July 1896.
28 See 26 above. Roderick Dhu was the fierce Highland chief of Sir Walter Scott's 'Lady of the Lake'.
29 *Stockport Advertiser*, 22 September 1916. From appreciation by 'An old Bramhall resident', published, with other tributes, after Charles Nevill's death.
30 *Daily Express*, 15 September 1916.

Chapter 8   The Hall in danger

1 e.g. *Country Life* (supplement), 26 November 1921; *The Times*, 16 May 1922; *Manchester Guardian*, 7 July 1923.
2 9 November.
3 Catalogue of sale, p. 4.
4 *Stockport Advertiser*, 13 July 1923.
5 *The Times*, 2 & 6 May 1925.
6 ibid., 28 May 1925.
7 *Stockport Advertiser*, 29 May, 5 & 19 June, 3 & 24 July 1925. See also *Manchester Guardian*, *The Times*, 29 May 1925.
8 *Daily Dispatch*, *Manchester Evening News*, 6 August 1925; *Manchester Guardian*, *Manchester Evening Chronicle*, 7 August 1925. See also (among others) *Stockport Advertiser* ('Bramall Hall spared'), *The Times* ('Preservation assured'), 7 August 1925.
9 *Lays and Legends of Cheshire*, pp. 92–3.
10 Conveyance, Mrs Amy Davies to Hazel Grove & Bramhall Urban District Council, 7 October 1935.
11 *Stockport Advertiser*, 4 November 1927.

Chapter 9   The treasures of Bramall Hall

1 14 May 1937.
2 Earwaker, p. 450.
3 Chas H. Nevill to Alfred Burton, 11 November 1887; from a copy made by Reginald Dean c. 1945 with note: 'Original letter pasted in [Burton's] Manuscript Book "The Township", folio 11'.

4   *Bramall Hall.* Concerning the chapel this single-sheet guide also states, 'The curious windows opposite the door were uncovered about two years ago'. A copy in Stockport Reference Library is dated 1891, but a handwritten note shows that it was still being used (by 'the Lady Caretaker') in June 1925. A reprint in different type and without date would seem to have been issued by Mr or Mrs Davies.

5   *Stockport Advertiser*, 29 April 1938.

6   ibid., 23 April 1937.

7   ibid., 1 April 1938.

8   ibid., from 'By the Way – Wayfarer'.

9   ibid., 4 November 1938, from 'In and Out of Doors'.

10 p. 443.

11 M. H. Ridgway, 'Coloured Window Glass in Cheshire, Part 2, 1400–1550', in *Trans. Lancs. & Ches. Antiquarian Society*, vol. 60 (1948), p. 70.

12 *The Davenport Heraldic Tapestry at Bramall Hall* (1955), p. 4.

13 *The Manor*, p. 813; *Manchester Courier*, 2 May 1877.

14 Various models of Bramall Hall were made in the 19th century. (See *The Manor*, pp. 1006, 1099). For description of model given to J. W. H. Davenport see *Alderley & Wilmslow Advertiser*, 22 July 1876. A model presented in 1887 by the Women of Stockport to Queen Victoria is now on display in the Swiss Cottage, Osborne House Estate, Isle of Wight.

15 L. Eveline Dean, *Davenport Portraits through the Ages* (typescript, 1950).

Chapter 10   The Hall as history

1   Vol. 65 (1955), p. 140.

2   *Stockport Advertiser* (supplement), 1 July 1887. See also Burton's articles 'Bramall Hall and its owners, 1 and 2' in *Stockport Advertiser* (supplements, Cheshire Notes and Queries, new series 76 & 78), 24 June and 8 July 1887.

LIST OF PRINCIPAL SOURCES

The Burton Manuscripts (referred to as *Domestic Architecture, The Manor,* and *The Township*)

Domestic Architecture of Lancashire and Cheshire (spine stamped *Ancient Domestic Architecture, Part 1*)

A History of Bramhall in the County of Chester,
vol. 1, *The Manor and its Owners*
vol. 2, *The Township*

Alfred Burton left a number of manuscripts, these three (undated but c. 1880–90) becoming the property of Charles Nevill (his name being written on the fly-leaves).
In 1936 they were given by Charles Nevill's nephew to the Hazel Grove & Bramhall Urban District Council and they are now the property of the Stockport Metropolitan Borough Council. They consist of articles and references copied from many sources, *The Manor* and *The Township* being interspersed with Burton's own notes on Bramall Hall and the village of Bramhall.

The Papers, Notes and Illustrations Collection of Reginald Dean

The Davenport Papers in the Cheshire Record Office, including, Sermon preached at the funeral of William Davenport, 1696 (DDA/1533/32); Administration and Inventory of William Davenport, 1696 (WS 1696); Wills of William Davenport, 1706 (WS 1706), John Davenport, 1722 (DDA), Warren Davenport, 1749 (WS 1749), William Davenport, 1820 (WS 1829), William Davenport Davenport, 1857 with codicil 1868 (WR 10 fo.295); Abstract of Title of John William Handley Davenport, 1877 (DDA/1384/203/5).

Catalogues of Sale:

Bramhall Hall, Cheshire, Catalogue of the highly valuable Household Appointments, Library of Books, &c. (1877)

Bramall Hall, Bramhall, Cheshire, Catalogue of an important six days' sale of fine old furniture . . . on Monday July 9th 1923 and five following days . . .

Bramall Hall estate . . . by auction at the White Lion Hotel, Stockport, on Tuesday, 21st July, 1925

Abstract of Title to Bramall Hall of the Stockport Metropolitan Borough Council

Hazel Grove & Bramhall Urban District Council, *Minutes*

Friends of Bramall Hall, *Minutes*

Printed accounts:

J. P. Earwaker, *East Cheshire; past and present; or a history of the hundred of Macclesfield . . . from original records*, vol. 1 (1877), pp. 422–455 Bramhall Township and Bramhall Hall

Hazel Grove & Bramhall Urban District Council, *Bramall Hall* (1950, revised c. 1958)
This 32-page brochure, which was in print until 1966, was written by Reginald Dean, the author's name appearing at the foot of page 31.

INDEX

Female members of the Davenport family, whether members by birth, marriage or adoption, are entered under the surname DAVENPORT

Stockport Metropolitan Borough
Council, x, 7, 104, 115
Stockport Parish Church, 7, 17-18, 21,
31, 37, 46
Stockport Savings Bank, 39
STORRS, Caleb, 34, 109n.17
STORRS, Elizabeth, 109n.17
Strines Printing Works, 62
SWINDELL, *Councillor* Frank, 101,
P1.20 (second left)
signature of, P1.19

Tarriff Reform Movement, 74
TATE, *Sir* Henry, 83
TATE, William, 34
TATTON, Robert, 100
TAYLOR, Henry, 3
TAYLOR, *Rev. J.*, 46
Territorials, The, 79
Timbers and timber framing, 3-4, 5,
6, 7, 8, 10, 22, 65, 68, 69, 91
Timothy's Quest, 74
TIPPING, William, M.P., 51
Torrington Diaries, quoted, 35-6
'Tub, The', 77

United States of America, 38-9, 71,
80

'Veronica', 77-8
Victoria, 63
Victoria & Albert Museum, 92-3, 104
Village hall, 75

Walker & Homfrays Ltd, 84
Wallbank Hill, 47, 110n.14
WARREN, *Sir* Edward (brother of
Dame Dorothy Davenport),
20, 22-3
WARREN, Edward (brother of
Margaret Davenport), 31
WARREN, John (father of Dame
Dorothy Davenport), 20, 22-3, 100
WARREN, John (father of Margaret
Davenport), 30

WARREN, Margaret (mother of
Dame Dorothy Davenport),
20, 22-3, 100
White Bank House, 79
*Widowed, or Where is my lord the
king?*, 89
WIGGIN, Kate Douglas, 71-4, 80
WILLIAMSON, Frederick Augustus,
46-7
Wills and inventories, 17-18, 30-1,
31-3, 34, 40, 46-7, 48, 85
WILSON, Sydney F., 87
WILSON, Shirley, 87
Windows, 4, 6, 7, 8, 9, 35-6, 65-6,
67, 72, 91
Withdrawing room, 9-10, 22, 35-6,
56, 65, 96, 97, P1.15
Wood carving, 4, 6, 7, 22, 55, 57,
60, 96, P1.3, P1.7
Woodford, 25, 79
Worksop, 108n.11
WORTH, Jasper, 21
WRIGLEY, Charles Harold, 2,
89-93, 96
signature of, P1.19
WRIGLEY, George, 91